AF600143

THE CATHOLIC UNIVERSITY OF AMERICA
CANON LAW STUDIES
No. 40

THE RESERVATION
OF THE
BLESSED SACRAMENT

A DISSERTATION

Submitted to the Faculty of Canon Law of the Catholic University of America in partial fulfillment of the requirements for the Degree of Doctor of Canon and Roman Law

---

BY

WILLIAM THOMAS CAVANAUGH, C. P., J. U. L.
(of the Province of St. Paul of the Cross)
Union City, N. J.

The Catholic University of America
Washington, D. C.
1927

Nihil Obstat:

CYPRIANUS MCGARVEY, C.P.
Censor Deputatus
Union City, N. J. die 4 Aprilis, 1927

Imprimatur:

STANISLAUS GRENNAN, C.P.
Praep. Provincialis.
Union City, N. J., die 4 Aprilis, 1927

Nihil Obstat:

✠ THOMAS J. SHAHAN, S.T.D.
Censor Deputatus
Washingtonii, D. C., die 9 Aprilis, 1927.

Imprimatur:

✠ MICHAEL J. CURLEY
Archiepiscopus Baltimorensis.
Baltimorae, die 9 Aprilis, 1927.

COPYRIGHTED 1927, BY S. GRENNAN

Printed by THE SIGN PRESS, *Union City, N. J.*

FOREWORD

The Reservation of the Blessed Sacrament is one of the oldest practices in the Church. The history of this practice, therefore, is an interesting expression of the teaching and practising faith of the Church in this august Sacrament.

In the pages that follow the history of the Reservation of the Blessed Sacrament shall be confined to the legislative action of the Church as it affects the *custodia* of the Sacrament. This legislation is found scattered throughout the enactments of General and Particular Councils, Constitutions of the Popes, and is crystallized in the Code of Canon Law.

The changes in the Code from the older discipline are very few. In the main, it repeats the legislation on the Reservation of the Blessed Sacrament that is, in many cases, centuries old. Because of the greater importance that the antiquity of the legislation gives to its modern expression in the Code, the older decrees on various points have been introduced. For the sake of completeness, decrees of the Sacred Congregations on matters not directly touched by the Code, but which are still in force as part of Liturgical Law, have been added.

CONTENTS

THE RESERVATION OF THE BLESSED SACRAMENT

INTRODUCTION

THE reason for the scrupulous care that the Church takes in its legislation on the Reservation of the Blessed Sacrament is to be found in her faith in the Real Presence of Christ in the Holy Eucharist and in the permanence of that Presence as long as the Sacred Species remain incorrupt. That Faith is thus expressed by the Council of Trent: *Principio docet sancta synodus et aperte et simpliciter profitetur, in almo sanctae Eucharistiae sacramento post panis et vini consecrationem Dominum nostrum Jesum Christum, verum Deum atque hominem vere, realiter ac substantialiter sub specie illarum rerum sensibilium contineri. Si quis negaverit in sanctissimae Eucharistiae sacramento contineri vere, realiter et substantialiter corpus et sanguinem una cum anima et divinitate Domini nostri Jesu Christi, ac perinde totum Christum, sed dixerit tantum esse in eo ut in signo, vel figura, aut virtute: anathema sit.*[1]

In regard to the permanence of the Real Presence of Christ in the Holy Eucharist, the same Council defined the following: *Si quis dixerit, peracta consecratione, in admirabili Eucharistiae sacramento non esse corpus et sanguinem Domini nostri Jesu Christi, sed tantum in usu, dum sumitur, non autem ante vel post, et in hostiis seu particulis consecratis, quae post communionem reservantur vel supersunt, non remanere verum corpus Domini: anathema sit.*[2]

1. Conc. Trid., sess. XIII, *de Eucharistia*, c. I; can. 1.
2. Ibid., sess. XIII, *de Eucharistia*, can. IV; cf also can. VII.

CHAPTER I.

THE PURPOSE OF RESERVING THE BLESSED SACRAMENT

THAT the Reservation of the Blessed Sacrament is one of the oldest practices in the Church, is a matter of historical fact; and is clearly evidenced by the testimony of the earliest of the Church Fathers. The chief reasons for this practice in the early Church are fundamentally the same as those that obtain today. But besides the more important reasons for the Reservation, we find others of a more or less symbolical nature. These latter will be outlined here, as merely of historical interest.

I. EULOGIA

The word *Eulogia* had two very different significations in the early Church. Sometimes it was used to designate the bread that was blessed at Mass and which the faithful received instead of Holy Communion. But the older use of the word applied it to the Particles consecrated at the Mass of the Pope or Bishop and sent to the neighboring priests as a sign of the latters' communion with their leaders.[1]

Pope Innocent I refers to this latter practice, in one of his letters. *De fermento, vero, quod die dominica per titulos mittimus, superflue nos consulere voluisti, cum omnes ecclesiae nostrae intra civitatem sint constitutae, quarum presbyteri, quia die ipsa propter plebem sibi creditam nobiscum convenire non possunt, idcirco fermentum a nobis confectum per acolythos accipiunt, ut se a nostra communione, maxime illa die non judicent separatos. Quod per parochias fieri debere non puto quia nec longe portanda sunt sacramenta: nec nos per coemeteria diversa constitutis presbyteris destinamus, et presbyteri eorum conficiendorum ius habeant atque licentiam.*[2]

1. *Militiades* [311] *fecit ut oblationes consecratis per ecclesias ex consecratu episcopi dirigentur, quod declaratur fermentum.* Duchesne, *Liber Pontificalis*, p. 168; Rock, Hierurgia, I. p. 261.

2. Ep. I. n. 5, Mansi, III, 1030; Bona, *Rerum Liturgicarum*, lib. I, cap. XXIII, p. 189.

The practice that the Pope had decided to limit by this letter was in use among the Bishops, also in those early days. They were wont to send particles consecrated at their Masses to the priests who were to celebrate in the *tituli*. It was also to be sent to the priests who celebrated the Paschal ceremonies.[3]

II. IN THE CONSECRATION OF ALTARS

About the ninth century a very unique practice arose in England and thence spread throughout Europe namely, the putting the Blessed Sacrament in the altars together with the relics or even alone when relics could not be had for the consecration of the altars. The following decree of the Synod of Chelsea [816] is the oldest one on the point: *Secundo. . . Postea Eucharistia quae ab Episcopo per idem ministerium consecratur cum aliis reliquiis condatur in capsula, ac servetur in eadem basilica. Et si alias reliquias intimare non potest, tamen hoc maxime proficere potest, quia corpus et sanguis est Domini nostri Jesu Christi.*[4]

From England the practice spread to the continent and soon found its way into the prescriptions of many of the Councils and Pontificals as obligatory in the consecration of altars even when relics were obtainable. This practice lasted until the fifteenth century.[5]

III. RESERVATION OF THE BLESSED SACRAMENT BY NEWLY-CONSECRATED BISHOPS AND VIRGINS

In the *Ordo Romanus VIII* there is a rubric that required a newly-consecrated Bishop to reserve the Blessed Sacrament,

---

3. Muratori, *Liturgia Romana Vetus*, I, 280; Bona, *Rerum Liturgicarum*, p. 193; Duschesne, *Christian Worship*, p. 185; Freeland, "The Reservation of the Blessed Sacrament," in, *Catholic Faith in the Holy Eucharist*, p. 155.

4. Mansi, XIV, 356; Pasqualigo, *De Sacrificio Novae Legis*, I, quaest. 679; Rock, *The Church of Our Fathers*, I, p. 35; Braun, *Der Christliche Altar*, I, p. 623; *Archiv fur Katholisches Kirchenrecht*, vol. 102 (1922) pp. 33-41.

5. Benedict VIII, Ep. 35, M., *P. L., CXXXIX*, 1633; *Text of the Dedication of the Church of St. Major*, Migne, *P. L., CLI*, 275; *Exordium Magnum Ordinis Cisterciensis*, dist. III, cap. XXII, Migne, *P. L., CLXXXV*, 1082; Braun, op. cit., pp. 623-629; Rock, *loc. cit.*, *Archiv fur Katholisches Kirchenrecht*, *loc. cit.*

consecrated at the Mass of his own consecration, so that he might communicate from It for the following forty days.[6]

Virgins, on the day of their consecration, received a large Host from which they were to communicate themselves for the following eight days. This practice continued until the twelfth century.[7]

IV. THE HOLY EUCHARIST BURIED WITH THE DEAD

There are few things in the history of the reservation of the Blessed Sacrament so surprising as the practice of burying It with the dead. It was certainly an abuse rather than a method of reserving the Holy Eucharist. What purpose such a practice was to serve, it is hard to see, unless it was done from a misunderstanding or an extension of the meaning of the Holy Viaticum. Whatever the reason, some of the earliest Councils in the Church condemned the abuse. Thus the First Council of Carthage: *"Item placuit, ut corporibus defunctorum Eucharistia non detur, scriptum est enim: 'Accipite et edite': cadavera vero nec accipere possunt nec edere."*[8]

This practice was also condemned by many other provincial Councils.[9]

V. THE UNITY AND IDENTITY OF THE MASS SIGNIFIED BY A RESERVED PARTICLE

The *Ordo Romanus I,* in describing the Mass of the Roman Pontiff, mentions a ceremony that can only be explained by the supposition that a consecrated particle was reserved from one Mass to the next for the fulfilment of this rubric: n. 18, *Cum dixerit 'Pax Domini sit semper vobiscum; faciens crucem tribus vicibus manu sua super calicem, mittit Sancta in eum.* The word *Sancta* here means the Holy Eucharist as is shown by

6. *Dum vero venerit ad communicandum, domnus apostolicus porrigit ei formatam atque sacratam oblationem; et eam suscipiens episcopus ipse ex ea communicat super altare, et sibi caeterum ex ea reservat ad communicandum usque ad dies quadraginta. . . .Ordo Romanus VIII,* n. 9,—Migne, *P. L.,* LXXVIII, 1004; Bona, *Rerum Liturgicarum,* lib. I, cap. XXIII, p. 193.

7. Martene, *De Ant. Eccl. Rit.,* lib. I, cap. V, art. 1, n. 5.

8. Mansi, III, 719; Muratori, *Liturgia Romana Vetus,* I, 283.

9. Conc. Carth. III, can. V, Mansi, III, 880; Conc. Hippon. can. V, Mansi, III, 895; Conc. Antissiod., Muratori, *loc. cit.*

its use in n. 8: *Et tunc duo acolythi tenentes capsas cum Sanctis apertas, et subdiaconus sequens cum ipsis tenens manum suam in ore capsae, ostendit Sancta Pontifici vel diacono qui praecesserit. . . .* It is also clear that the Pontiff dropped a consecrated Particle into the Precious Blood before he broke the Host consecrated at the Mass he was saying. This latter was not done until after he had completed the other ceremony, as n. 19 shows: *Tunc Pontifex rumpit oblatam ex latere dextro; et particulam, quam rumpit, super altare reliquit: reliquias vero oblationes suas ponit in patenam.*

Further evidence that the Blessed Sacrament was reserved from one Mass to another is to be found in n. 22. If the Pontiff could not be present at the *statio*, the Bishop who celebrated Mass in his place was to drop into the chalice a Particle that was consecrated by the Pontiff. *Quando dici debet 'Pax Domini sit semper vobiscum,' deportatur a subdiacono oblationario particula fermenti, quod ab Apostolico consecratum est, et datur archidiacono, ille vero porrigit Episcopo.*[10]

The *Ordo* further prescribes the same ceremonies for priests and Bishops in general. *Similiter etiam et a presbytero agitur, quando in statione facit Missas, praeter Gloria in Excelsis Deo: quia a presbytero non dicitur nisi in Pascha. Episcopi, qui civitatibus praesident, ut summus Pontifex, ita omnia peragunt.*[11]

This suggests the Reservation of the Blessed Sacrament for the Mass of the Pre-Sanctified, but as the modern discipline on this Reservation does not differ substantially from the ancient practice, its consideration will be treated later.

VI. RESERVATION OF THE BLESSED SACRAMENT FOR THE SICK.

The purpose of the earliest legislation on the Reservation was to provide the sick and the dying with the Holy Viaticum. Thus the First Council of Nice enacted the following decree: *De his qui ad exitum veniunt, etiam nunc lex antiqua regular-*

10. *Ordo Rom.* V, in Muratori, *Liturgia Romana Vetus*, II, 978, 984, 988; Mabillon, *Museum Italicum*, II, *In Ordinem Romanum*, pp. XXXV & CXLII; *Eglogae Amalarii Abbatis in Ordinem Romanum*, in *Museum Italicum*, n. VI, p. 550.

11. *Ordo Rom.* I, n. 22 *in fine*.

isque servabitur; ita ut si quis egreditur e corpore, ultimo et maxime necessario viatico minime privetur.[12]

This canon was not new legislation, but a recognition of an obligation already existing in virtue of a custom and was an incorporation of this custom into the written law of the Church. It did not directly require the reservation of the Blessed Sacrament, but, in ordering that the sick should not be deprived of Viaticum, it implied the necessity of the reservation of It for this purpose. This interpretation of the decree of Nice is based on these words of the Council of Trent: *Consuetudo asservandi in sacrario sanctam Eucharistiam adeo antiqua est, ut eam saeculum etiam Nicaeni concilii agnoverit.*[13]

In keeping with the obligation of providing for the sick and dying, as required by the Council of Nice, this purpose is especially insisted upon from the very beginning, in the decrees of various particular Councils.[14]

The regulations of these Councils and many others were recognized by the Council of Trent: *Consuetudo asservandi in sacrario sanctam Eucharistiam adeo antiqua est, ut eam saeculum Nicaeni Concilii agnoverit. Porro deferri ipsam sacram Eucharistiam ad infirmos, et in hunc usum diligenter in ecclesiis conservari, praeterquam quod cum summa aequitate et ratione coniunctum est, tum multis in conciliis praeceptum invenitur, et vetustissimo catholicae ecclesiae more est observatum. Quare haec Synodus retinendum omnino salutarem hunc et necessarium morem statuit.*[15]

The reservation of the Blessed Sacrament for the sick was, therefore, the main reason for the practice and made that practice universal in the Church. The other reasons for the reservation of the Blessed Sacrament were not so generally prevalent nor were they insisted upon by the different Councils of the Church in ordering the keeping of the Holy Eucharist.

---

12. Can. XIII, *Fontes*, n. 1.
13. Conc. Trid., sess. XIII, *de Eucharistia*, c. 6.
14. Tours (461), cap. IV, Mansi, VIII, 950; Synodal Statutes of Rheims (630), cap. IX, Mansi, X, 599; Statutes of St. Boniface, n. IV, Mansi, XII, 384v; Ancient Capitular, Mansi, XIII, 1083; Toledo (650), Mansi, X, 777; Egbert (748), Collection of Canons, n. XXII, Mansi, XII, 415; Capitula Rudolphi (850), cap. VI, Mansi, XIV, 947; Hincmar (858), cap. IV, Mansi, XV, 480; Capitulare Galterii, in Synod of Bouillon, cap. VII, Mansi, XV, 506; Capitula Herardi, n. LVI, Mansi, XVIIIB, 1289.
15. Conc. Trid., sess. XII, *de Eucharistia*, c. 6.

Gradually also there grew up around the Holy Eucharist, a devotion that gave added reason for Its reservation for the spiritual benefit of the faithful in general. Slowly but very surely the ancient practice of frequent Communion was being renewed in the Church and the satisfying of the people's desire for this Heavenly Food gave another reason for the reservation of the Blessed Sacrament.

This reason, though weighty enough, is, however, a secondary one, the principal reason still being that the sick and dying may not be deprived of Holy Viaticum.[16]

16. Canons 864, §1; 1270; Cavalieri, *Rituale Expensum*, p. 223; *Gasparri*. *Tractatus de SS. Eucharistia*, II, p. 248.

CHAPTER II.

CONDITIONS FOR THE RESERVATION OF THE BLESSED SACRAMENT

CANON 1265 §1. *Sanctissima Eucharistia, dummodo adsit qui eius curam habeat et regulariter sacerdos semel saltem in hebdomada missam in sacro loco celebret*: 1°. *etc.*

In this clause of Canon 1265, there are set down two conditions that must be assured wherever the Blessed Sacrament *must* or *may* be reserved. First, there must be a custodian to take care of the Blessed Sacrament by seeing that the regulations regarding Its proper reservation are observed and by protecting It from all danger of irreverence; and, secondly, Mass must be said in the church or oratory where It is reserved, at least once a week. The introduction of the clause by the word *dummodo* makes these conditions indispensable.[1]

Without the fulfilment of these conditions, the Blessed Sacrament may not be reserved. The position of this clause in the first paragraph of the canon which regards only cathedrals, parish churches and the public or semi-public oratories of religious and pious institutes, gives rise to the question of its application to the churches and oratories mentioned in the second paragraph. As regards the habitual reservation of the Blessed Sacrament in these churches and oratories, there is no difficulty, because the necessary Apostolic indult makes provision for all the requisites for the proper custody of It, as will be seen later on. Where the local Ordinary uses the faculty given him by this paragraph to permit the temporary reservation of the Blessed Sacrament in these churches and oratories, the proper care of the Eucharist, which is one of his chief concerns, will prompt him to take the conditions set down in the first paragraph as a guide in allowing this temporary reservation of the Blessed Sacrament.

1. Barbosa. *Tractatus Varii. Dictiones Usufr.* v. dummodo, *dictio* XCV.

I. THE CUSTODIAN OF THE BLESSED SACRAMENT

In the early days of the Church the responsibility for the protection of the Holy Eucharist against irreverence rested on those who kept It in their homes for the private reception of Holy Communion. Solicitude for the reverence due to this Sacrament was one of the reasons why Tertullian opposed the marriage of a Christian with a pagan. Such marriages made it very difficult for the Catholic to guard the Holy Eucharist from irreverence. On the other hand, one of his reasons for commending Catholic marriages was that both parties can partake of the Body of the Lord together at home.[2]

All the danger of irreverence did not, however, have its source in the paganism of the time. Christians themselves were often unmindful of the sanctity of the august Presence in the Eucharist.

A common practice was to apply the Sacred Host to the body of a sick person to obain his cure. Thus, Gorgonia, the sister of St. Gregory Nazianzen, arose one night in a sickness and "applied the Body and Blood of Christ to her head and chest and received immediate relief."[3] The faith of Gorgonia may be praised but the practice was carried to such an extent as to lead to many abuses. St. Augustine relates how some went so far as to make poultices of the Blessed Sacrament.[4]

Finally heretics, mingling with the faithful, received the Blessed Sacrament and, instead of consuming It, sacrilegiously used It for various evil purposes.[5]

These irreverences led many particular Councils in the early Church not only to forbid lay people and sometimes even subdeacons to take the Sacred Host, but even to enter the *sacrarium,* where the Holy Eucharist was reserved, or to touch the sacred vessels. The effect of these prohibitions was to leave the care of the Blessed Sacrament to deacons and priests. Thus the Council of Braga (572) forbade laics to enter the room where the Blessed Sacrament was kept.[6]

The Eighteenth Council of Toledo (694) forbids minis-

2. *Ad Uxorem,* lib. II. Migne. *P. L.,* I. 1296, 1303.
3. St. Gregory Nazianz. *Oratio VIII, In Laudem Sororis suae Gorgoniae,* Migne, *P. G.,* XXXV. 810.
4. *Contra Julianum,* III. n. 162, Migne, *P. L.,* XLV, 1315.
5. Petra, *Comm. ad Const. Apost., Const. I Urbani IV,* sec. un. n. 5.
6. Can. XLII, Mansi, IX, 855.

ters, i. e. all those not deacons, to touch the sacred vessels or even to enter the sacristy.[7]

Again, Odo, Bishop of Paris, required the rectors of the churches to see to it that the greatest reverence and honor be shown the sacred altars and especially the one where the Holy Eucharist is reserved.[8]

By the time of the Fourth Lateran Council, it was the general practice that the only custodian of the Blessed Sacrament could be a priest. A decree of this Council placing the penalty of suspension on carelessness in regard to the custody of the Holy Eucharist certainly restricted this office to a cleric. *Si vero is, ad quem spectat custodia, ea incaute dereliquerit, tribus mensibus ab officio suspendatur, et si per eius incuriam aliquid nefandum contigerit, graviori subjaceat ultioni.*[9]

Pope Honorius III, however, leaves no doubt that only priests are to be the custodians of the Blessed Sacrament. *Ne de cetero propter incuriam sacerdotis in indevotos divina indignatio gravius exardescat districte praecipiendo mandamus, quatenus a sacerdotibus in loco singulari, mundo etiam, et signato semper honorifice collocata, devote ac fideliter conservetur.*[10]

By this command the care of the Holy Eucharist is not only a privilege reserved to priests but also a matter of strict obligation. There is nothing to indicate that this care might be left to lay persons. On the other hand, the nature of the penalty imposed for carelessness was such as only a priest could incur.

After the establishment of the Sacred Congregations, the necessity of providing for the presence of a priest where the Blessed Sacrament was to be reserved, and to serve as Its custo-

---

7. Sententia XIX. *Quoniam non oportet ministros licentiam habere in secretario, quod Graeci "diaconoecon" appellant, ingredi et contingere vasa dominica.*

Sententia XVIII. . . .*Similiter autem honorificetur diaconus a ministris inferioribus et omnibus clericis.* Mansi, XII, 107; cf. also Mansi, XII, 867; XVIIIB, 1287.

8. Cap. V, *de Sacramento Altaris,* n. 5,. . . .*Ut rectores ecclesiarum et presbyteri videant, ut summa reverentia et honor maximus sacris altaribus exhibeatur et maxime ubi sacrosanctum Corpus Domini reservatur et missa celebratur.*" Mansi, XXII, 677.

9. C. 1, X, *de custodia Eucharistiae, chrismatis et aliorum sacramentorum,* III, 44; Pignatelli, *Consultationes Canonicae,* tom. IV, cons. XXXI.

10. C. 10, X, *de celebratione Missarum, et sacramento Eucharistiae et divinis officiis,* III, 41.

dian, is more clearly and definitely declared in their decrees, and especially in those of the Sacred Congregation of Rites.

Thus on March 23, 1593, this Congregation gave the following response on the occasion of the erection of a church by the Baron named therein: *Ad petitionem Rudolphi Baronis Cat. de Boluailler censuit, si Sanctissimo Domino nostro placuerit, ex speciali privilegio posse concedi, ut in ecclesia. . . .possit asservari Sanctissimum Eucharistiae Sacramentum. . . dummodo ecclesia ipsa sit decens, et solita conferri in titulum, et nunc habeat beneficiatum perpetuum qui eius curam gerat, et Sacramentum possit caute custodiri.*[11]

Again, in another decree of the same Sacred Congregation, March 16, 1833, it was required that the priest in charge of a church where the Holy Eucharist was reserved either reside near it himself, or, if he was to be absent for some time, he was to get another priest to take his place while he was away. The question asked was: *An aedituus ruralis ecclesiae, ubi Sanctissimum Eucharistiae Sacramentum semper asservatur, teneatur ibi residere, ut Sacrosanctum missae Sacrificium quotidie celebret; vel possit per quinque aut sex dies quolibet mense abscedere ut aliis obligationibus in alia ecclesia vacet?* The reply of the Sacred Congregation was: *Teneri ad residentiam et quotidianam missae celebrationem, per se vel per alium sacerdotem.*[12]

It is true that the custody of the Blessed Sacrament is not the only reason for the obligation of residence. But in the question that was here proposed, the reservation of the Blessed Sacrament is made the basis for the question on residence and on the daily celebration of Mass. And the answer of the Sacred Congregation makes the custody of the Blessed Sacrament one of the reasons for the residence of the priest and the daily Mass. Indults for the reservation of the Blessed Sacrament in other than parochial churches were never granted unless there was a priest present to care for It.[13]

However, the Holy See departed from its usual practice of requiring the residence of a priest as the custodian of the Blessed Sacrament in an indult granted to the Daughters of Charity of

11. Decr. Auth., n. 31.

12. Decr. Auth., n. 2700.

13. Petra, *Comm ad Const. I Urbani IV*, n. 37; Gatticus, *De Domesticis Oratoriis*, cap. XVIII, n. X & XI; Gasparri, *De SS. Eucharistia*, II, p. 261.

St. Vincent de Paul. This grant is contained in the following words of the Apostolic Letter, *Caritatis Viscera*, of Gregory XVI: *Motu proprio, ac certa scientia, matura deliberatione atque apostolicae potestatis plenitudine concedimus et indulgemus, ut in aedibus Filiarum Charitatis ubique positis, dummodo initi saltem numero quinque sint contubernales, vel secus plures puellae institutionis causa penes eas degant, sacellum possit haberi, decenter tamen ornatum et ab omnibus domesticis usibus liberum atque ab Episcopo prius de more invisendum, ibique super ara, quae necessaria supellectili pro dignitate sit instructa, libere liciteque sanctissimum Eucharistiae sacramentum possit asservari; cum lege quidem ut ante tabernaculum, quo divina hostia continetur, diu noctuque lampas alatur; utque eius tabernaculi clavis maneat penes sacristam sive aedituum, qui fida, illam, custodia tueatur. Concedimus praeterea, ut in ipso sacello, quatenus in una eademque domo simile privilegium nequaquam vigeat, ea episcopi venia et arbitrio, in singulos dies, etiam solemniores, a quocumque presbytero rite probato sacrificium fieri possit.*[14]

Besides the ordinary conditions of a fitting tabernacle, becoming ornaments and a lamp, it is required that there be at least five Sisters or several girls living in the house, and this, wherever the institute has houses, though the favor was asked only for those of France. In virtue of this letter, the Sisters were really made the custodians of the Blessed Sacrament, without the necessity of having a resident chaplain, as the answer to the following doubt on this very letter shows: *Attentis Litteris Apostolicis*, 2°: *An in eiusmodi oratoriis strictim privatis asservari queat Sanctissimum Eucharistiae Sacramentum, minime obstante quod in annexa ecclesia idem Sanctissimum Sacramentum in tabernaculo iugiter custodiatur? Et quatenus affirmative*, 3°: *An tolerari possit quod in eiusmodi privatis oratoriis Sanctissima Eucharistia diu noctuque servetur absque sacerdote ibidem commorante, solis Sororibus veluti concredita?* The Sacred Congregation of Rites replied: Ad 2: *Affirmative;* Ad 3 *Affirmative; servatis conditionibus in Apostolico Breve contentis.*[15]

Another indication of change in the earlier legislation re-

---

14. Gregory XVI, *Caritatis Viscera*, May 14, 1833, *Acta Gregorii Papae XVI, I*, n. CCXXV, p. 252.

15. S. R. C., May 8, 1886, Decr. Auth., n. 3662.

quiring the residence of a priest wherever the Blessed Sacrament was to be reserved, is found in a decision of the Sacred Congregation of Rites on a doubt proposed to it in 1881. After forbidding the practice of leaving the Blessed Sacrament wrapped in a corporal on the floor of the tabernacle, to avoid the sacrilegious theft of the sacred vessels, it added this admonition: *Dum itaque huiusmodi rescriptum communicatur, Reverendissimum Episcopum monere praestat ut provideat quatenus in quavis ecclesia, ubi Sanctissimum Sacramentum retinetur, numquam desit custos, qui prope eam commoretur, prouti ab ecclesiasticis praescriptionibus sancitum est.*[16]

In regard to this admonition it is to be noted that while all the other decrees used the term *sacerdos* in speaking of the custodian of the Blessed Sacrament, here the more general term *custos* is used.[17]

Such a change in terminology in the decrees, with the uniformity in the express use of the word *sacerdos* in the older ones, and the use of the more indefinite term *custos* in this one, permits the conclusion that the general custody of the Holy Eucharist might be entrusted to others than priests.

The Code also avoids the use of any expression in this canon that would indicate that the custodian of the Holy Eucharist is to be a priest. It requires only that there be someone present who will have the care of It. Relying, then, on the two decrees last quoted as indicative of a mitigation of the severity of the ancient obligation that the custodian of the Blessed Sacrament should be no one but a priest, and the fact that the Code does not stress the older discipline, it may be said that the custodian of the Blessed Sacrament need not always be a priest. The Blessed Sacrament may be kept in churches or oratories even though there is not a priest present as the custodian, provided someone else fulfils this office.[18]

The fact that the Code today allows the reservation of the Blessed Sacrament, where formerly an Apostolic Indult was necessary, and also that it is well known that most places have no resident chaplain, makes this explanation of the Canon pos-

16. S. R. C., Feb. 17, 1881, Decr. Auth., n. 3527.

17. Cf. Petra, *op. cit.*, n. 38.

18. Vermeersch-Creusen, *Epitome*, II, n. 588; Fanfani, *De Jure Parochorum*, p. 237; Woywod, in *Homiletic and Pastoral Review*, XXXVII, n. 1, p. 36; Augustine, *Commentary*, VI, p. 215.

sible. However, Blat requires what will generally be the case when a lay person is the custodian of the Blessed Sacrament, namely, that the custody be *sub ductu sacerdotis.*[19]

The priest who says the Mass, required by this canon, in the oratory where the Blessed Sacrament is reserved will be able to make any corrections in the proper custody of It, when and if these become necessary.

Cappello, however, maintains that the custody of the Holy Eucharist may only be given to priests.[20]

Though the decree that he quotes allows only a priest to be the custodian of the Blessed Sacrament, the indult to the Daughters of Charity and the decree of 1881, both later than the one he quotes, permit the broader interpretation of the first clause of this canon. Furthermore, the effect of the restriction of this clause to mean only priests would make the privilege of reserving the Blessed Sacrament in many of the churches and oratories mentioned in the second section of this paragraph practically useless.

In particular, the custodian of the Blessed Sacrament in parochial churches will be the pastor: *Parochus summum studium in eo ponat, ut ipse venerabile Sacramentum, qua decet reverentia, debitoque cultu. . . .custodiat.*[21]

If the parish is attached to a collegiate church or to one belonging to a religious community, the chapter or the community, respectively, is the custodian of the Blessed Sacrament.[22] In this case, a key to the tabernacle is to be given to the one that has the actual care of souls, so that he may at all times be able to discharge his obligations to them without inconvenience.[23]

In the churches or oratories of lay religious communities, hospitals, orphanages and other Catholic institutions where the local Ordinary allows the reservation of the Blessed Sacrament, the community, as such, is Its custodian, unless a resident chaplain is appointed[24]

It is rarely, if ever, permitted to reserve the Blessed Sacra-

---

19. *Comm. Text. C. I. C.*, lib. III, pars III, n. 133.
20. *De Sacramentis*, I, pp. 249-250.
21. Rit. Rom., tit. IV, cap. 1, *de sanctissimo Eucharistiae sacramento*, n. 2; cf. *Acta Eccl. Mediol.*, pars, IV, p. 513.
22. Canons 415, §3, n. 1; 609, §1.
23. Canon 415, §3, n. 1.
24. Augustine, *Commentary*, VI, p. 216: *Il Monitore Ecclesiastico*, Series IV, vol. II, p. 19.

ment in private oratories because of the dangers of irreverence. When an indult is granted to do so, it contains special provisions for the proper custody of the Holy Eucharist.[25]

Supervision of the proper custody of the Blessed Sacrament in the non-exempt churches of his district is one of the rights and obligations of the Vicar Forane. He is to see that there is fitting splendor in these churches, according to their means, and that there is proper cleanliness especially in regard to the reservation of the Blessed Sacrament and the celebration of Mass.[26]

In the pastoral visitation of the churches of the diocese the Bishop is also to see that the proper care is exercised in reserving the Blessed Sacrament. Thus in the Council of Trent it was decreed: *"Quaecumque in diocoesi ad Dei cultum spectant ab Ordinario diligenter curari atque iis, ubi oportet, provideri aequum est."*[27]

The same obligation has been included in the Code in Canon 336. There can be no doubt that the proper care of the Blessed Sacrament is included here because everything connected with this Sacrament deals directly with the worship of God Who is really and truly present in it. In the rubrics for visiting parishes, after the absolution of the dead, the Bishop begins the visitation of the church with an inspection of everything pertaining to the reservation of the Blessed Sacrament.[28]

Not only are secular churches subject to this visitation but also the churches of religious congregations even though the individual congregation may be otherwise exempt.[29]

It is not so clear that the Bishop may visit the parochial churches of Regulars that are attached to the monastery and belong to them. Before the Code, these were subject to this visitation of the Bishop who acted in this matter as the delegate of the Holy See. But wherever the Code speaks of the visitation of the religious pastor, it speaks only of a personal visitation and not of a local visitation. And in regard to the reservation

25. Petra, *op. cit.*, n. 37.
26. Canon 447, §1. n. 4; Blat, *De Personis*, p. 479.
27. Conc. Trid., sess. XXI, *de reformatione*, c. VIII.
28. Pontificale Romanum, *Ordo ad Visitandas Parochias*; Caeremoniale Episcoporum, lib. I, c. VI, n. 2; *Ecclesiastical Review*, Supplement, May, 1897.
29. Canon 512, §2, n. 2.

of the Blessed Sacrament, in particular, there seems to be no doubt that the Bishop cannot make the visitation of It. The custody of the Blessed Sacrament belongs to the community which is exempt by law from the jurisdiction of the Bishop and therefore cannot be visited by him.

Many of the commentators on the Code, confusing the personal visitation of the pastor and the local visitation of the church, say that the Bishop can make the visitation of the latter. Canon 344, §1 establishes the presumption that all ecclesiastical places in the diocese are subject to the episcopal visitation unless they are expressly exempted by law. Canon 615 expressly exempts the churches of Regulars from the jurisdiction of the Bishop and by inference from a visitation by him. It is clear, however, that in the only two places where the Code speaks of the visitation of the religious pastor, it is contemplating only a personal visitation.

Therefore, the conclusion seems to be justified that the churches of Regulars that are also parochial are not subject to the episcopal visitation in regard to the reservation of the Blessed Sacrament. If abuses should creep in in this regard, the Bishop is to admonish the Superior in order that he may remove them and if the latter is negligent, the Bishop is to inform the Holy See.[30]

A summary of this section shows that the Blessed Sacrament was kept privately by the faithful in the early Church, thus placing the responsibility for Its proper care on lay people. When they ceased to show the reverence due to It and when heretics began to treat It sacrilegiously, Its custody was committed to no one but a priest. So necessary was the residence of a priest wherever the Blessed Sacrament was reserved that, without it, this reservation was forbidden. This discipline prevailed until the nineteenth century when an indult was granted to the Daughters of Charity throughout the world permitting the reservation of the Blessed Sacrament with the Sisters as Its custodians. And in providing for the proper re-

---

30. Canons 631, §1: 1425, §2: Benedict XIV, const. "*Firmandis*," Nov. 6, 1744, §§7-10, *Fontes*, n. 349; Barbosa, *Summa Apost. Decis.*, coll. CCCXXV, n. 16; Giraldi, *Expositio Juris Pontificii*, I, p. 446; Lucidi, *De Visitatione Sacrorum Liminum*, I, p. 93; Vermeersch-Creusen, *Epitome*, II, n. 581, 2°; Fanfani, *De Jure Parochorum*, p. 360; Id., *De Jure Religiosorum*, p. 453; Blat, *De Personis*, n. 570; Wernz-Vidal, *De Personis*, pp. 640 & 791-792.

servation of the Blessed Sacrament on another occasion the protection of the Blessed Sacrament from thieves was to be obtained by a *custos* to live near the church. This more indefinite designation of some one who will have care of the Blessed Sacrament is used by the Code, making it permissible to reserve the Blessed Sacrament in a church or oratory even though there is no resident priest nearby. The observance of the second condition for the reservation of the Blessed Sacrament, viz. the celebration of Mass at least once a week, will provide for the renewal of the Hosts and give the opportunity for the correction of anything that may not be done properly. In this way, too, the *ductus sacerdotis* that Blat mentions would also be assured.

II. THE CELEBRATION OF MASS ONCE A WEEK

As there is a departure in the Code from the former discipline in regard to the custodian of the Blessed Sacrament, there is also a change in the requirement for the frequency of the Mass to be said in the churches and oratories in which the Blessed Sacrament is reserved. It was ordinarily required before the Code that Mass be said every day in such churches and oratories. Now it is required that Mass be said regularly at least once a week.

That the general practice required Mass every day wherever the Blessed Sacrament was reserved, is clear from the decree of the Sacred Congregation of Rites that was quoted above.[31]

The priest in charge of the church where the Holy Eucharist was reserved was obliged not only to residence but also to daily celebration of Mass in the church. If he were absent only five or six days of a month, he was to have another priest to take his place and say the Mass. And a decree of the Sacred Congregation of the Council forbade the reservation of the Blessed Sacrament in rural churches where Mass was said only on feast days.[32]

The Sacred Congregation of Rites, in response to a question asked of it, forbade the reservation of the Blessed Sacrament in a hospital because Mass was not said there on feast days. *An in nosocomio Papien. permitti valeat in uno ex duobus*

31. March 16, 1833. Decr. Auth., n. 2700.
32. Petra, *Comm. ad Const. I Urbani IV*, n. 30.

sacellis ibi existentibus Sanctissimum Eucharistiae Sacramentum servetur, etsi in eo nec omnibus diebus festivis Sacrum peragatur; vel prohiberi id omnino debeat, non obstante periculo cui subessent infirmi moriendi absque Sanctissimo Viatico ob incommodum satis grave pro sacerdote adeundi alterum sacellum ut inde sacra Synaxis iisdem procuretur? The Sacred Congregation replied: *Negative, et ad mentem: Mens est ut sacerdos ex proximo sacello sumat Sanctissimam Eucharistiam eamque deferat infra pectus capsula inclusam.*[33]

In this response there was question of Mass being said only on feast days, and nothing is said at all of Mass every day in the chapel. From this decision it would seem that there was a mitigation of the older prescription of daily Mass in churches and oratories where the Blessed Sacrament was reserved.

This is confirmed from another decision of the same Congregation given on May 14, 1889. If Mass could not be said every day in oratories that had the privilege of reserving the Blessed Sacrament in virtue of an Apostolic Indult, another indult was to be asked of the Sacred Congregation which was accustomed to require that Mass be said at least once a week. *I. Num permitti possit quod Sanctissimum Sacramentum asservetur in praefatis oratoriis, quamvis nec semel in hebdomada ibi missa celebretur? Et quatenus negative, II. Quoties in hebdomada celebrari debeat missa? An semel tantum sufficiat; et an interdici debeat asservatio, si bis per hebdomadam missa celebrari nequeat?* The reply was: *Ad I, Negative; Ad II, Si in iis oratoriis missa quotidie celebrari nequit, ab Apostolica Sede indultum petendum est, quae semel saltem in hebdomada illam praecipere solet.*[34]

Such indults, as this reply indicates, were still exceptions to the general rule, but in the light of the former severity with which the daily celebration of Mass was required, they suggest a changing of conditions that would warrant the reservation of the Blessed Sacrament when Mass could be said only once a week. But in 1890, a decision was given which indicates that the celebration of Mass once a week in these churches and oratories was becoming more and more the general practice and the practice was given a tacit recognition by the Sacred Congrega-

33. Nov. 23, 1880, Decr. Auth., n. 3525 ad III.
34. May 14, 1889, Decr. Auth., n. 3706.

tion of Rites. The Archbishop of Compostella proposed a doubt on reserving the Blessed Sacrament in filial churches where the Blessed Sacrament was reserved although Mass was said there only on Sundays and the doors were not left open during the week. The Sacred Congregation of Rites forbade the reservation of the Blessed Sacrament if the doors were not left open and did not make any reference to the fact that Mass was said once a week.[35]

To-day the Code plainly requires that Mass be said at least once a week. As this is to be done regularly, an accidental omission of the Mass would not interfere with this regularity.[36]

Neither need the Mass be said at the altar of the Blessed Sacrament. It is merely required that it be said in the sacred place.[37]

35. Nov. 15, 1890, ad I, Decr. Auth., n. 3739.

36. Vermeersch-Creusen, *Epitome*, II, p. 342; Cappello, *op. cit.*, I, p. 249.

37. Blat, *Comm. Text. C. I. C.* lib. III, pars III, n. 133.

Canon 1265. §1. *Sanctissima Eucharistia,. . . .*

1°. *Custodiri debet in ecclesia cathedrali, in ecclesia principe Abbatiae vel Praelaturae nullius, Vicaritus et Praefecturae Apostolicae, in qualibet ecclesia paroeciali et in ecclesia adnexa domui religiosorum exemptorum sive virorum sive mulierum.*

2°. *Custodiri potest, de licentia Ordinarii loci, in ecclesia collegiata, et in oratorio principali sive publico sive semipublico tum domus piae aut religiosae, tum collegii ecclesiastici quod a clericis saecularibus vel a religiosis regatur.*

§2. *Ut in aliis ecclesiis seu oratoriis custodiri possit, necessarium est indultum apostolicum; loci Ordinarius hanc licentiam concedere potest tantummodo ecclesiae aut oratorio publico ex iusta causa et per modum actus.*

§3. *Nemini licet sanctissimam Eucharistiam apud se retinere aut secum in itinere deferre.*

Canon 1266. *Ecclesiae in quibus sanctissima Eucharistia asservatur, praesertim paroeciales, quotidie per aliquot saltem horas fidelibus pateant.*

Canon 1267. *Revocato quolibet contrario privilegio, in ipsa religiosa vel pia domo sanctissima Eucharistia custodiri nequit, nisi vel in ecclesia vel in principali oratorio; nec apud moniales intra chorum vel septa monasterii.*

CHAPTER III

THE PLACES WHERE THE BLESSED SACRAMENT IS RESERVED

I. CHURCHES OBLIGED TO RESERVE THE BLESSED SACRAMENT

WHAT has been said in the first chapter on the purposes for which the Blessed Sacrament is reserved today, namely, that the sick may not die without Viaticum and that the other faithful may have the opportunity to receive Holy Communion, gives us the sources of the obligation to reserve the Holy Eucharist. Cathedral churches, the principal churches of Abbacies and Prelatures Nullius, Vicariates and Prefectures Apostolic, all parochial churches and the churches attached to the houses of exempt Religious, whether men or women, must all reserve the Blessed Sacrament.

(A). CATHEDRAL CHURCHES.

Prior to the Code, the obligation to reserve the Blessed Sacrament in cathedrals, when they did not have the care of souls attached to them, arose only from custom. The *Caeremoniale Episcoporum* gave consideration to this custom in the following regulation on the altar of the Blessed Sacrament: *Quod [altare, scil., ubi est Sanctissimum Sacramentum] diversum esse solet ab altari maiore et ab eo in quo Episcopus, vel alius est missam solemnem celebraturus.*[1]

But there was nowhere any obligation in written law for the reservation of the Blessed Sacrament in these churches. Canonists generally spoke of cathedrals as being permitted to reserve the Blessed Sacrament because they were the primary parishes of the diocese, even though they may not have been parishes in the strict sense of having the care of souls. It was not so much an obligation, therefore, as a privilege extended to

1. Lib. I. cap. XII. n. 8.

them for this reason, and that from a favorable interpretation of the law.[2] But for this same reason that the cathedral was the first parish of the diocese, some maintained that the reservation of the Blessed Sacrament in it was obligatory.[3] In the province of Milan, it was obligatory from a decree of a provincial council.[4]

Whatever may have been the reason for which the Blessed Sacrament was reserved in these churches, whether by an extension of the term "parish" so as to make it a privilege or an obligation, there can be no doubt now that the Blessed Sacrament must be reserved in them even though there is no parish attached to them. It seems sufficient reason that the noblest church in the diocese should be the residence of our Sacramental Lord.[5]

If two dioceses are united *aeque principaliter*, that is, without any change in the status of either and with neither of them subjected to the other, the Blessed Sacrament must be reserved in both of them.[6] Each remaining a cathedral in its own right, retains its own privileges, prerogatives and obligations. Therefore, the Blessed Sacrament may and must be reserved in each. Any other union of the dioceses leaves the obligation only on the superseding cathedral in an extinctive union, and on the principal cathedral in a subjective or accessory union.[7]

(B). Parochial Churches.

A parochial church is the church designated as belonging to a territorial part of the diocese. Each church has a determinated group of people and a proper pastor. A quasi-parochial church is the church of a similar territorial division of a Vicariate or Prefecture Apostolic. National parishes are recognized in law as real parishes, though they serve only a particular class of people, the distinction being generally based on language, and their churches are parochial.[8]

2. Petra, *Comm. ad Const. I Urbani IV*, n. 15; Many, *Praelectiones de Missa*, p. 276; Gasparri, *op. cit.* II, p. 251; Van der Stappen, *Sacra Liturgia*, IV, p. 106; Cappello, *De Visitatione SS. Liminum et Dioeceseon*, I, p. 150.
3. Lucidi, *De Visitatione Sacrorum Liminum*, I, p. 94.
4. *Acta Eccl. Mediol.*, Conc. I, pars I, p. 8.
5. Blat, *op. cit.*, lib. III, pars III, p. 161.
6. Canon 1419, 2°
7. Cappello, *De Visitatione SS. Liminum et Dioeceseon*, I, pp. 719-720; *De Sacramentis*, I, p. 250.
8. Canon 216.

The antiquity of the obligation for the reservation of the Blessed Sacrament in parochial churches was seen in the decrees of the early Councils quoted in the first chapter. The obligation of the faithful to receive Holy Viaticum when they are in the danger of death, with the resulting duty of those having the care of souls to administer It to them, made the reservation of the Blessed Sacrament in parochial churches a necessity.[9]

As was seen above, in the very early days of the Church, the faithful provided for the reception of Holy Viaticum by reserving the Blessed Sacrament in their homes. The danger of being led to death at anytime during the Persecutions made this custom a necessity, and especially as the Christians never knew when they would be deprived of their priests during those times. Then, too, the practice of receiving Holy Communion devotionally at home was another reason for this private reservation of the Blessed Sacrament. With the cessation of the Persecutions, however, the fervor of the people began to cool. The result was that they were forbidden to take the Blessed Sacrament home with them and priests were commanded to provide for their needs in this matter by keeping It in the church.[10]

The obligation to reserve the Blessed Sacrament rests upon every pastor. No parochial or quasi-parochial church is exempt from this. If, however, the income of the parish is insufficient for the proper reservation of the Sacrament, the Sacred Congregation of the Council, in 1604, allowed the Bishop to have the Blessed Sacrament reserved in one of the parish churches of a region, with the others contributing what they could to the decorous reservation. *Eucharistiae sacramentum quando in omnibus parochialibus Montanae Regionis asservari pro tenuitate redituum nequit, episcopus decernere debet ut in singulas ternas quaternasque vicinas parochiales id onus distributatur, ut in una ex eis habeatur augustissimum Sacramentum et ad impensam lampidis et huiusmodi ceterae vicinae contribuant, illa-*

9. Conc. Nicaen. I. can. 13. *Fontes* n. 1; Canon 864; c. 93. D. II. de cons.; Rit. Rom. tit. IV, cap. 1, *de sanctissimo Eucharistiae sacramento*, n. 5; Many, *op. cit.*, p. 275; Noldin, *Theol. Mor.*, III, p. 156; Augustine, *Commentary*, IV, pp. 242-243; Cappello, *De Sacramentis*, I, p. 247.

10. Tertullian, *Ad Uxorem*, lib. II, Migne, *P. L.*, I, 1296; St. Basil, *Ep. ad Caesar.*, XCIII, Migne, *P. G.*, XXXII, 483; Eusebius, *Hist. Eccl.* lib. IV, c. 44, Migne, *P. G.*, XX, 630; Conc. Tolet. I. Mansi, III, 634; Conc. Caesaraugust., Mansi, III, 1000; Many, *op. cit.*, p. 274.

que, ubi se casus obtulerit, perinde uti rectores possint ac si in propria parochiali illud asservaretur.[11]

The financial inability to reserve the Blessed Sacrament in a parochial church was declared an insufficient reason for the suppression or transfer of a parish, by the same Sacred Congregation in a decree of August 17, 1697. Some parishes had been suppressed and transferred by reason of their poverty and the opposition to these acts was proposed to the Congregation of the Council in the following questions: 1°. *An translatio ecclesiarum parochialium facta sustineatur; et quatenus negative*: 2°, *An in iisdem ecclesiis parochialibus sit asservandum sanctissimum Eucharistiae sacramentum.* The reply was: *Ad I, Negative; ad II, ad mentem.* The mind of the Sacred Congregation was that, pending other arrangements to be made by the Bishop, the pastors were to continue their practice of getting the Holy Viaticum from the cathedral or some other church reserving the Blessed Sacrament.[12]

Moreover, the Sacred Congregation of Bishops and Regulars, in a decree of March 14, 1614, required the reservation of the Blessed Sacrament in every parish church *quantumvis paupere; quod si redditus, et societas non sufficiat, instituatur quaestor, vel eleemosynarum collector.* By this decision, the appointment of one who was to collect alms for the purpose was made an ordinary means of providing sufficient income for the parish church to fulfil its obligation to reserve the Blessed Sacrament becomingly.[13]

In missionary countries, if the Blessed Sacrament cannot be kept in the church, or if the place where Catholics worship is also used by non-Catholics, It is to be kept in the house of the pastor or some other priest. *Quando missionarius non potest decenter servare Eucharistiam quia in ecclesia non sunt nec ianuae nec fenestrae, quaeritur utrum possit, vel debeat, servare Eucharistiam, sint infirmi vel non. Resp. Detur Instructio ad Helvetios 3 Augusti* 1803.—*'Ad impediendum quamcumque erga res sacras irreverentiam, S. C. censuit non expedire ut a catholicis in sacrario communi cum protestantibus retineatur oleum sanctum, sacrum chrisma et sanctissima Eucharistia; sed vult ut*

11. Petra, *Comm. ad Const. I, Urbani IV*, n. 27.
12. Petra, *loc. cit.*
13. Cavalieri, *Rituale Expensum*, p. 223.

haec omnia asserventur in loco separato ab acatholicis; et si alius locus proprius non habeatur, asserventur potius cum omni possibili decentia in domo parochi vel alterius sacerdotis.'[14]

In very extensive parishes, filial or mission churches are often built for the convenience of those who live in the outlying parts of the parish. Similarly, in the Summer time, there are many chapels within parish limits for the convenience of transients. There is no obligation to reserve the Blessed Sacrament in these churches as they are not properly parochial. They are in reality extensions or annexes of the parish church and serve temporarily the needs of the people living near them. To avoid the danger of irreverence that may arise from having to carry the Blessed Sacrament a long way in a hurry, it is advisable that the Blessed Sacrament be reserved in these churches. The permission to do so can be granted by the Bishop.[15] When the permission to reserve the Blessed Sacrament in these churches is granted, provision is to be made for someone to look after It. There is generally no question about the Mass being said once a week, because these churches are built for the purpose of giving the people an oportunity to hear Mass on Sunday and holydays.

(C). THE CHURCHES OF EXEMPT RELIGIOUS.

The reservation of the Blessed Sacrament, which is now obligatory on exempt Religious, whether of solemn or simple vows, was formerly considered by some as being solely permissable,[16] while others considered it strictly obligatory.[17]

Two reasons are given for this reservation of the Blessed Sacrament by exempt Religious. First, by their exemption, they are placed outside the jurisdiction of the Bishops and pastors in this matter, thus being constituted, as it were, a parish with the necessity of providing for their own spiritual needs. Secondly, before the Code, they were said to enjoy the right to

14. Coll. S. C. de Prop. Fide, n. 1079; Gasparri, *op. cit.*, II, p. 250; cf. Formula Facultatum S. C. de Prop. Fide, form. III, (A), n. 14, in Vermeersch-Creusen, *Epitome*, I, p. 487.

15. Pont. Comm. ad Int. C. I. C., May, 20, 1923, A. A. S., XVI, p. 115; Petra, *op. cit.*, n. 28; Gasparri, *op. cit.*, II, p. 250.

16. Petra, *op. cit.*, n. 18; Cavalieri, *Rituale Expensum*, p. 223; Gasparri, *op. cit.*, *II*, p. 251; Many, *Praelectiones de Missa*, p. 277; Cappello, *De Visitatione SS. Liminum et Dioeseseon*, I, p. 151; Vermeersch-Creusen, *Epitome*, II, p. 342.

17. Wernz, *Jus Decretalium*, III, p. 554; Martinucci, *Manuale Decretorum*, p. 619, note.

reserve the Blessed Sacrament in virtue of a tacit privilege granted by the Holy See. The foundation for this is to be found in the following decree of the Sacred Congregation of Rites: *Moniales SS. Annunciationis de Bastia supplicarunt pro facultate asservandi in earum ecclesia Sanctissiman Eucharistiam. Et S. R. C. respondit; Aut monasterium est canonice erectum, et non indiget: aut non, et non est approbandum.*[18]

This response, in the absence of any law requiring exempt Religious to reserve the Blessed Sacrament, can be understood in no other way than as either a recognition of a custom in the matter or a tacit privilege.

Though the Blessed Sacrament must be reserved in the churches or principal oratories of the houses of Regulars, whether clerical or lay, and of those Religious who have exemption by grant of the Holy See, it is necessary also today that the house be canonically erected, as this decree requires.[19]

The Holy Eucharist must be reserved by the Religious whether the house is a *domus formata* or *non-formata*. As the latter class is under the particular vigilance of the local Ordinary, he himself may correct any abuses in regard to the reservation of the Blessed Sacrament there.[20]

Nuns, that is, those religious women who belong to an institute which by its rules has solemn vows, though *de facto* the members may not have them, because of various circumstances, are obliged to reserve the Blessed Sacrament provided they are at the same time subject to a Regular Superior in accordance with the Code. Only such nuns have some measure of exemption.[21] They are obliged to reserve the Blessed Sacrament even though for the time being they do not enjoy this exemption, as is the case in some countries at present owing to political conditions.[22]

---

18. April 16, 1664, Decr. Auth., n. 860; Cappello, *De Visitatione*, I, p. 151; Lucidi, *De Visitatione SS. Liminum*, I, p. 94.

19. Canons 615, 618; Augustine, *Commentary*, VI, p. 214; Vermeersch-Creusen, *Epitome*, II, p. 342.

20. Canons 488, 5°; 617, §2; cf. Instr. S. Paenit. Apr. 18, 1867 ad IV, in Vermeersch, *De Religiosis*, Suppl. II, p. 313. This instruction permitted the reservation of the Blessed Sacrament in houses where only four priests were living. The Code does not make this restriction. Cappello, *De Sacramentis*, I, p. 248.

21. Canon 615.

22. Vermeersch-Creusen, *Epitome*, II, p. 342; Blat, *Comm. Text. C. I. C.*, lib. III, pars III, p. 161.

However, in religious houses where the Blessed Sacrament is kept either because of this obligation or from the permission of the local Ordinary, as will be seen presently, It may be kept only in the church or principal oratory, and nuns may not reserve It within the cloister, every privilege to the contrary being revoked.[23] The latter part of this canon is almost a verbatim repitition of a decree of the Council of Trent on this point. *Quod vero sanctissimum Christi corpus intra chorum vel septa monasterii, et non in publica ecclesia conservetur, prohibet sancta synodus, non obstante quocumque indulto aut privilegio.*[24] The reason for this is to be found in the law of the cloister, which does not permit any priest to enter the enclosure for the purpose of saying Mass or to renew the Sacred Species, both of which are necessary in the proper reservation of the Blessed Sacrament.

Canon 1267 contains two prohibitions concerning: (a) the number of tabernacles for all Religious, (b) the location of the altar of the Blessed Sacrament in the houses of nuns.

(a). Concerning the first prohibition, the following doubt was proposed for solution to the Pontifical Commission for the Authentic Interpretation of the Code: 1°. *Canon* 1267, *quo statuitur in religiosa vel in pia domo Sanctissimam Eucharistiam custodiri non posse nisi vel in ecclesia vel in principali oratorio, intelligendusne est ita, ut prohibeatur eam custodiri praeterquam in publica ecclesia pro commoditate fidelium, etiam in principali oratorio, in quod sodales conveniunt ad exercitia pietatis communia? Et quatenus negative ad primum*:

2°. *An idem dicendum sit, si quando ecclesia clausa ordinarie maneat et fidelibus non pateat.*

3°. *An idem dicendum sit de pluribus oratoriis in eadem pia domo pluribus sodalium classibus destinatis (duobus, vel tribus, etc., pro novitiis ex gr., fratribus laicis, studentibus, sacerdotibus) ita ut unaquaeque classis suum distinctum habere possit oratorium cum Sanctissimo Sacramento; an potius hoc coarctandum ad ecclesiam et oratorium pro tota communitate destinatum.*

RESP.: *Sensus canonis* 1267 *hic est. Si religiosa vel pia domus adnexam habeat publicam ecclesiam eaque utatur ad or-*

23. Canon 1267.
24. Conc. Trid., sess. XXV, *de regularibus*, c. 10.

dinaria et quotidiana pietatis exercitia explenda, Sanctissimum Sacramentum in ea tantum asservari potest; secus in oratorio principali eiusdem religiosae vel piae domus (sine praeiudicio iuris ecclesiae, si quod habet) ; *in eoque tantum, nisi in eodem materiali aedificio sint distinctae ac separatae familiae, ita ut formaliter sint distinctae religiosae vel piae domus.*[25]

From this it is clear that if the community goes to the church for its daily spiritual exercises, the Blessed Sacrament may be kept there only and not in the principal oratory.[26] If the community is a formal unit and goes to the principal oratory and not to the church for its daily spiritual exercises in common, the Blessed Sacrament may be reserved in that oratory and also in the church if the community has the right to reserve It there in virtue of Canon 1265, §1, n. 1. If it has not that right but reserves the Blessed Sacrament only because of the permission granted according to n. 2 of that canon, It may be kept only in the oratory where they have their spiritual exercises.[27]

Finally, if there are formally distinct communities in the one house, i. e. formally distinct in government, administration and in their exercises of piety,[28] as for example, the students in a seminary and the Sisters in charge of the domestic arrangements, the Blessed Sacrament may be reserved in the principal oratory of each community. Whether this extends so far that the Blessed Sacrament may be reserved in one oratory for the novices and another for the professed members of a community when both are in the same building, is not so clear. A writer in the *Il Monitore Ecclesiastico,* in a note attached to this decision by way of commentary, would allow it.[29] Vermeersch and Blat, however, think this to be an excessive extension of the decision.[30]

The solution of the difficulty seems to be in whether or not the novices or other group within the community attend the same spiritual exercises or use the same oratory. If they do,

25. June 2-3, 1918, A. A. S., X, p. 346.

26. Vermeersch-Creusen, *Epitome,* II, p. 344; Blat, *op. cit.,* lib. III, pars III, p. 163.

27. Blat, *op. cit.,* p. 164.

28. Blat, *loc. cit.*

29. Series III, vol. X, p. 236.

30. *Epitome,* II, p. 344; *Comm. Text. C. I. C., loc. cit.;* cf also Fanfani, *De Jure Religiosorum,* p. 414.

then as far as the exercises of piety are concerned, they are subject to the regulations of the local Superior, because these exercises of piety are, in the supposition, a matter of the discipline for the whole house. In this matter, therefore, they would not constitute a formally distinct class. And the multiplication of the places where the Blessed Sacrament is reserved is not justified. But if any of these classes has its own oratory and performs its own spiritual exercises independently of any other group, then the Blessed Sacrament may be reserved in as many chapels as there are independent groups.

(b). The second prohibition in Canon 1267 forbids the reservation of the Blessed Sacrament within the cloister of nuns. The reason for this has already been stated. In Spain, some communities of nuns, besides keeping the Blessed Sacrament on the altar of the public church, also had an arrangement in the wall between the sanctuary and their chapel so that the Blessed Sacrament might be kept there and a priest, by removing a slide, could expose the Blessed Sacrament for the adoration of the nuns. This was done in order to evade the prohibition to reserve It within the cloister, as decreed by the Council of Trent. The Holy See forbade the practice to be continued in Spain or to be introduced elsewhere.[31] The Sacred Congregation of Rites in a response given on December 2, 1885, declared, however, that a similar practice could be tolerated in the chapel of the Colletines at Cambrai.[32]

In rural houses belonging to exempt religious and kept either for the purpose of having a place where their sick members may go for their health or for the sake of recreation, it was formerly forbidden to reserve the Blessed Sacrament without an Apostolic Indult.[33] And when the Fathers of the Oratory applied to the Sacred Congregation of the Council for an indult to reserve the Blessed Sacrament in one of their rural houses in Portugal, where some of the Fathers had gone for their health and others for recreation, the greatest difficulty arose before it was granted. But considering the fact that the place was used by the sick and on the favorable word of the Nuncio to Lisbon,

31. Pignatelli, *Consultationes Canonicae*, tom. VIII, cons. LII.

32. Decr. Auth., n. 3648.

33. Petra, *op. cit.*, n. 23; Gasparri, *op. cit.*, II, p. 251; Many, *Praelectiones de Missa*, p. 277.

the indult was granted for seven years.[34] Resting on this decision, some maintain that an indult is also required after the Code in order that the Blessed Sacrament may be reserved in these rural houses.[35] But as the canon does not distinguish between a rural house and others, the Blessed Sacrament may be kept in the former as well as in the latter, as long as it is canonically erected into a religious house.[36]

II. CHURCHES AND ORATORIES REQUIRING THE PERMISSION OF THE BISHOP TO RESERVE THE BLESSED SACRAMENT.

A collegiate church is one to which there is attached a college of clerics, or chapter, for the purpose of giving solemn worship to God.[37]

The public oratory of a pious or religious house, or of a college is that oratory erected primarily for the use of these groups but to which all the faithful have the proved right to go for Divine services. If only some of the faithful may attend it, the oratory is semi-public.[38]

A religious house in this section of the Canon 1265, is a canonically erected house of any non-exempt religious community whether of men or women, and also the houses of those without vows who live a life formed after the fashion of the religious life. A pious house is one devoted to religious or charitable works, such as orphanages, hospitals and the like, where priests or religious exercise the spiritual care. According to Vermeersch, schools and colleges in which priests or Religious have the spiritual care also come under the heading of pious houses, while an ecclesiastical college is an institution where young men are trained for the secular or religious priesthood.[39]

The Blessed Sacrament may be reserved in the churches or oratories of these places only with the permission of the local Ordinary. Formerly, the granting of this permission was re-

---

34. S. C. C., in *Ulissiponen.*, 3. Sept. 1707, in Petra, *loc. cit.*
35. Augustine, *Commentary*, VI, p. 215.
36. Cappello, *De Sacramentis*, I, p. 251.
37. Vermeersch-Creusen, *Epitome*, II, p. 272.
38. Canon 1188, §2, nn. 1 & 2.
39. S. C. pro Rel., Sept. 7. 1909, A. A. S., I, p. 700; Jan. 4. 1910, A. A. S., II, p. 63; Vermeersch-Creusen, *Epitome*, II, p. 342; Blat, *op. cit.*, lib. III, pars III, p. 161.

served to the Holy See exclusively.[40] This was clearly stated many times in the Pontifical Constitutions and decrees of the Sacred Congregations. Thus Benedict XIV in his Constitution, *Quanvis Justo*, of April 30, 1749, §24: *Sanctissimum Eucharistiae Sacramentum in ea (ecclesia) asservetur, pro qua asservatione Sanctitas Sua, cui id reservatum est, facultatem opportunam indulget Episcopo Augustano. Quod sane decretum a Nobis tunc viva voce approbatum, nunc eo libentius confirmamus, quod, et praefati Conservatorii Virgines debitam oboedientiam iam praestitisse, et pium, suique gregis vere amantem Episcopum Augustanum iam quoque illis indulsisse accepimus, ut in earum ecclesia, et Missae, ut prius celebrentur, et SS. Eucharistiae Sacramentum retineatur. Quoniam vero alterius huiusmodi gratiae concedendae ius ad Nos et Apostolicam Sedem privative pertinet, quod innuit Decretum superius relatum, et Canonica docet Disciplina, iuxta quam Sacrosancta Eucharistia in ecclesiis, quae parochiales non sunt, retineri non potest, absque praesidio Apostolici Indulti, vel immemorabilis consuetudinis, quae huiusmodi Indulti praesumptionem inducit; ut late ostenditur in Commentariis bon. mem. Cardinalis Vincentii Petra ad Romanorum Pontificum Constitutiones, et signanter ad Constit. I Urbani IV, sect. unic. num. 29 et sqq., tom. III.*[41]

The clarity with which this exclusive right of the Holy See to grant the permission to reserve the Blessed Sacrament in the churches other than parochial, is here vindicated, makes the quotation of decrees on the matter superfluous. They may be found in many of the older authors.[42]

Although the granting of this permission was thus reserved to the Holy See, there existed in some places a custom in virtue of which Bishops also had this faculty.[43] This privilege arose from a custom together with a prescription against the rights of the Holy See. There is no doubt that a privilege may be acquired by custom: *A consuetudine ad privilegium valet argu-*

---

40. Barbosa, *Collectanea Doctorum in Conc. Trid. ad sess. XIII, de SS. Eucharistia, c. VI*; petra. *op. cit.*, n. 24; Ferraris, *Bibliotheca*, v. *Eucharistia*, n. 45; Wernz, *Jus Decretalium*, III, n. 549; Gasparri, *op. cit.*, II, p. 252.

41. *Fontes*, n. 398: the decree referred to is one of the S. C. Epp. et Reg., July 21, 1748, in Bizzari, *Coll.*, p. 369.

42. Petra, *op. cit.*, nn. 24 & 29; Ferraris, *Bibliotheca*, v. *Eucharistia*, n. 45; Gasparri, *op. cit.*, II, pp. 252-253.

43. Many, *Praelectiones de Missa*, pp. 281-282.

mentum. Consuetudine enim introduci potest, quicquid per privilegium concedi valet.[44]

Added to this there was the question of prescription against the right of the Holy See, since the power to grant this permission to reserve the Blessed Sacrament in non-parochial churches was reserved solely to the Pope. For this prescription to be effective all the usual conditions were required including that of its being continued for one hundred years.[45] The validity of the use of this privilege depended on the fulfilment of all the conditions in the prescription.[46]

Under the present law, all the local Ordinaries may grant this permission for the reservation of the Blessed Sacrament in the Churches and oratories mentioned in this section of Canon 1265. The implicit permission of the Ordinary suffices for this, as in those cases where he exempts an institution from the care of the local pastor and appoints a chaplain to look after the spiritual needs there.[47]

This permission may be given to the Sisters in this country who teach in the parochial schools. Their houses are religious houses in the sense of this paragraph which does not distinguish between a *domus formata* and a *domus non-formata.* With them to safeguard the reverence due to the Blessed Sacrament and to take care of the chapel, provision need only be made for the celebration of Mass there once a week, in order that the permission may be given.

For all these communities, the Blessed Sacrament may be kept either in the church or in the principal oratory, but not in both. If they choose the principal oratory for their exercises of piety, they may not reserve the Blessed Sacrament in their church or public oratory, if they have one. Such communities have not the right in law to reserve the Blessed Sacrament as have those mentioned in the former part of this canon.[48]

---

44. Barbosa, *Tract. Varii, Tract. Locorum comm. Argumentorum* Iuris, loc. XXV, n. 2.

45. *Venerandae Romanae leges, divinitus per ora principum promulgatae, reum eius praescriptionem nonnisi per centum annos admittunt,* C. 17, c. XVI, q. 3; cf. c. 13, 14, X, *de praescriptionibus,* II, 26; c. 4, X, *de confirmatione utili vel inutili,* II, 30; Roelker, *Principles of Privilege,* pp. 59-66.

46. Cappello, *De Visitatione,* I, p. 152.

47. Canon 464, §2; Blat, *op. cit.* lib. III, pars III, p. 161.

48. Blat, *op. cit.,* lib. III, pars III, p. 164.

III. THE RESERVATION OF THE BLESSED SACRAMENT IN OTHER CHURCHES AND ORATORIES

The second paragraph of Canon 1265 determines the conditions under which the Blessed Sacrament may be reserved in all the churches and oratories not mentioned in the preceding sections of the canon. The chief ones to be considered are the oratories of confraternities and private oratories.

The traditional discipline of the Church on the reservation of the Blessed Sacrament in these churches and oratories is here restated. In fact, as was indicated before, an Apostolic Indult was necessary for the reservation of the Blessed Sacrament in all churches that were not parochial. The following doubt was proposed to the Sacred Congregation of the Council in 1609: *An episcopus possit concedere Ecclesiae non-parochiali, ut in ea retineatur Sanctissimum Sacramentum Eucharistiae solum pro adoratione, vel requiraturne auctoritas Papae; II, Praesupposito, quod Episcopus concesserit licentiam huiusmodi, an Episcopus successor dictam licentiam revocare possit?* The answer was: *Ad I. Huiusmodi licentiam fuisse nullam, ac propterea ei non esse deferendum, nec esse necessariam revocationem.*[49]

The reservation of the Blessed Sacrament in these churches was not for the purpose of providing Holy Viaticum for the sick as this right belongs exclusively to parochial churches. There is merely the question of reserving It for the adoration of the faithful, and the permission to do so can be obtained from the Holy See only. In granting this permission, the Holy See always adds clauses safeguarding the rights of the local pastor, and requiring the consent of the Bishop. But it is seldom if ever allowed to reserve the Blessed Sacrament in private oratories because of the danger of irreverence.[50]

Under the terms of this paragraph of Canon 1265 the Holy See alone can grant permission for habitual reservation of the Blessed Sacrament in these chapels and churches.[51] The

49. Petra, *op. cit.*, n. 30

50. Cf. Decr. Auth. nn. 31; 420; 895; 2123; 3484 ad III. This latter decree recalled and renewed the necessity for an indult of the Holy See for the reservation of the Blessed Sacrament not only in the churches here considered, but also for those of communities non-exempt, seminaries and in general all churches that were not parochial. Petra, *op. cit.*, n. 37.

51. Vermeersch-Creusen, *Epitome*, II, p. 343.

faculty of the local Ordinary is restricted to the allowing of the reservation of the Blessed Sacrament in non-parochial churches and public oratories. He can grant this permission only for a just cause and then only for a short time.[52]

Such cases would be the repairing of the parochial church, or the lack of seating capacity in a church which makes the use of another church or chapel necessary on Sunday. Whatever the cause, as long as it requires only the temporary reservation of the Blessed Sacrament outside of the church that must reserve It, this permission may be given.[53]

At this point, the question arises on the continuance and force of a custom to reserve the Blessed Sacrament in churches and oratories that have not the permission to do so by law or indult. The Sacred Congregation of the Council recognized the force of custom to this effect when it decreed: *Sanctissimum Eucharistiae Sacramentum asservandum est in uno loco cuiuscumque ecclesiae, in qua custodiri debet, potest aut* SOLET.[54]

Such a custom had value only if it produced the presumption of an Apostolic Indult. The first condition necessary for this presumption was that the custom had existed from time immemorial as Benedict XIV declared.[55] Secondly, there must be a putative title to allow the reservation of the Blessed Sacrament by custom. This title was created by the absence of proof of the existence of an invalid title. If it were certain that the custom of reserving the Blessed Sacrament began with the permission of the Bishop and rested on this alone, the custom could not be recognized because the very foundation of the custom was known to be faulty and recognition of it would imply the recognition of an insufficient and invalid title. It was in this sense that the Sacred Congregation of the Council refused to recognize such a custom in a decision given in 1609. On the other hand, if there were no proof of an invalid title and the custom were immemorial or a century old, or if only of forty years standing with a putative title productive of good

52. Ibidem.

53. Augustine, *Commentary*, VI, p. 217; Blat, *op. cit.*, lib. III, pars III, p. 162; Vermeersch-Creusen, *loc. cit.*

54. April 27, 1709, Cavalieri, *Rituale Expensum*, pp. 225-226; Giraldi, *Expositio Iuris Pontificii*, I, p. 447.

55. *Quamvis Justo*, §24, *Fontes*, n. 398.

faith from the beginning, the reservation of the Blessed Sacrament in virtue of such a custom could be continued.[56]

The customs to reserve the Blessed Sacrament contrary to this paragraph of the canon are not reprobated. Therefore there are some that had their origin before the Code that may be continued. The only ones are those that are immemorial or a century old, which the local Ordinary judges cannot be prudently abolished.[57]

All others of a shorter duration were revoked by the Code. For the custom to exist and have force after the Code, it must be general throughout a diocese or other subject of ecclesiastical law and forty years is sufficient as there is no express prohibition to the origin of any custom contrary to the prescription of this canon.[58]

Since Canon 26 declares that a custom may arise only in a community that can be the subject of laws, the practice of reserving the Blessed Sacrament in one or two churches or oratories of a diocese contrary to the regulation of Canon 1265, §2, would be a privilege dependent upon prescriptive right. But since this privilege can be obtained by an Apostolic Indult alone, it cannot be acquired by prescription.[59]

During the war, permission was granted, for the first time in history, for the reservation of the Blessed Sacrament in camp hospitals and on warships. *Sacra Congregatio de disciplina Sacramentorum, Illmi. ac Rmi. Ordinarii Castrensis in Italia precibus benigne annuens, vigore facultatum a Ssmo. D. N. Benedicto Papa XV tributarum, eidem committit ut durante praesenti bello, pro suo arbitrio et conscientia veniam faciat qua tum in stativis castrorum valetudinariis, tum in bellicis navibus ubi pro classiariis administer pró sacris adest, Ss. Eucharistiae Sacramentum adservari possit, dummodo altare, in quo ciborium collocabitur, sit decenter instructum et supellectilibus sufficienter praeditum; ibìdem sacrosanctum Missae sacrificium semel saltem in hebdomada celebretur, eiusdem ciborii clavis caute custodiatur; lampas ante Ss. Sacramentum collucescat; sacrae Species fre-*

---

56. S. C. C., *in Neapolitana*, 1609; July 2, 1707; July 28, 1708; Petra, *op. cit.*, nn. 31-35; Gasparri, *op. cit.*, II, p. 254; Cappelo, *De Visitatione*, I, p. 153, Many, *Praelectiones de Missa*, p. 281.

57. Canon. 5.

58. Canons 25-27; Cappello, *De Sacramentis*, I, 256-257.

59. Canon 1509, 2°.

quenter iuxta rubricas renoventur, aliisque servatis cautelis ipsi Ordinario Castrensi benevisis pro diversitate circumstantiarum et locorum, ad tutamen et decorem Ss. Eucharistiae. Contrariis quibuscumque minime obstantibus.[60]

IV. PRIVATE RESERVATION OF THE BLESSED SACRAMENT

As was pointed out before, the Persecutions made the private reservation of the Blessed Sacrament by the early Christians imperative in order that they might be able to receive Holy Viaticum if they were suddenly led away to death or deprived of their priests. They were also accustomed to take the Blessed Sacrament with them on journeys because of the dangers of traveling in those days. Thus St. Ambrose praised his brother's faith in the Holy Eucharist even before his conversion. "Before he was initiated in the more perfect mysteries, being in a ship-wreck, tossed about by the waves, not fearing death, but rather that he should be drowned without the Mystery, asked the Divine Sacrament of the faithful, from those whom he knew to be Christians, not that he might look on the hidden things with curious eyes, but that he might obtain the help of his faith. For he bound It in a stole, and put the stole about his neck."[61]

St. Basil also witnesses to the private reservation of the Blessed Sacrament, in a letter to Caesaria: "It is not necessary to show that in the time of the persecution, when no priest or deacon could be had, one received from his own hand, and the custom of to-day confirms this. For all the monks in the solitude where there is no priest, keep the Holy Communion in their cells and communicate themselves. However, in Alexandria and other parts of Egypt, all the people have Communion at home and, when they wish, partake of It.[62]

It was not long after the Persecutions that the custom began to die out of itself because of the cooling of the fervor of the early Christians and also because of the explicit prohibition of

---

60. June 22, 1915, A. A. S., VII, p. 329; Vermeersch, *Periodica,* VIII, pp. 278-279.

61. *De Excessu Fratris,* lib. I, Migne, *P. L.* XVI, 1304; Freeland, "Reservation of the Blessed Sacrament" in *Catholic Faith in the Holy Eucharist,* p. 155.

62. Ep. XCIII, ad Caesar., Migne, *P. G.,* XXXII, 483.

various Councils. That the devotion promoting the people to keep the Blessed Sacrament in their homes for Holy Communion, was fast disappearing, is clear from decrees that are found at the beginning of the sixth century requiring the reception of Holy Communion a certain number of times a year under penalty of not being considered Catholics.[63]

The prohibition to take the Blessed Sacrament from the church was made because of the many irreverences that were being committed against It by heretics who mingled with the faithful and took It away for unworthy purposes. The Council of Saragossa forbade any laic taking the Blessed Sacrament away under penalty of being anathema forever.[64] And the Council of Toledo (400) ordered that anyone who did not consume the Holy Eucharist on receiving It, was to be expelled as sacrilegious.[65]

To make it more difficult for the people to take the Blessed Sacrament home with them, the Council of Rouen (650) abolished, for that province, the custom then generally followed of putting the Blessed Sacrament into the hands of the faithful who then communicated themselves. Instead, it ordered that the priest put the Host into the mouth of the communicant as is our present custom. *Nullo autem laico aut feminae Eucharistiam in manibus ponat, tantum in os eius cum his verbis ponat . . . .Si quis haec transgressus fuerit, quia Deum omnipotentem contemnit, et quantum in ipso est inhonorat, ab altari removeatur.*[66]

There was, however, no general legislation forbidding this private reservation of the Blessed Sacrament or the carrying It on journeys. Thus, St. Boniface commanded his priests to carry the sacred chrism, holy oils and health-giving Eucharist with them wherever they went so as to be always prepared for their ministry.[67] And recently-consecrated virgins were permitted to retain the Holy Eucharist for devotional Communion

---

63. Conc. Agde., (506) can. XVIII, Mansi, VIII, 327; cf. also Autun (670), can. XIV, Mansi, XI, 126; Chalon-sur-Saone II, can. XLVII, Mansi, XIV, 103.

64. Art. III, can. 44, Mansi, III, 634.

65. Mansi, III, 1000; VIII, 1232.

66. Can. 2, Mansi, X, 1199.

67. Can. 4 Mansi: XII, 384v; cf. also *Ancient Capitular* (ca. 800), Mansi, XIII, 1083.

for eight days after their consecration as late as the twelfth century.[68]

The practice of private reservation of the Blessed Sacrament was gradually abolished, until the seventeenth century, when abuses were renewed by evil-minded men who took It for sacrilegious purposes. These abuses brought forth the severest penalties on those guilty of such crimes. And in order to prevent the sacrilegious acts every one was forbidden to take the Blessed Sacrament from the church. Innocent XI, in his Constitution, *Ad Nostri* Apostolatus, of March 12, 1677 gave the following decree. §1. *Auctoritate Apostolica statuimus, et decernimus, ut deinceps omnes, et singuli utriusque sexus, qui de furto Hostiae consecratae, sive unius, vel plurium particularum consecratarum cum Sacra Pyxide, vel sine illa per legitima iudicia iudicialiter iuxta S. Officii Inquisitionis contra haereticam pravitatem auctoritate Apostolica institute regulas, et praxim confessi, aut convicti fuerint, quive propria malitia, vel de alterius ordine, seu mandato hostiam, sive unam vel plures particulas consecratas praedictas apud se retinuerint, vel alio transferre, seu asportare praesumpserint condignis poenis, et animadversionibus pro facinoris atrocitate puniantur, et nisi constiterit non fuisse ad malum finem, etiam pro prima vice Curiae Saeculari tradantur, non obstante minore aetate, dummodo vigesimum attingat annum, quibus poenis etiam mandantes subiacent.*[69]

These crimes were so severely punished because they were considered as resulting from heretical opinions on the Real Presence. The perpetrators of such crimes were at least suspected of heresy and were punished accordingly. Moreover, the presumption seemed to be that the taking or retaining of the Blessed Sacrament was for a criminal purpose so that the only escape from punishment lay in proving that this malicious intent did not exist. Unless the accused did so to a certainty, he was to be punished even though it were his first offense. Alexander VIII, in his Constitution *Cum Alias* of December 22, 1690, renewed the prescriptions of the former constitution and added the penalties for such offenses were not to be condoned or lessened.[70]

68. Martene, *De Ant. Eccl. it.* libi, cap. V, art. I, n. V.
69. Fontes, n. 250.
70. Fontes, n. 255.

In spite of these severe regulations, there were delays in trials and mitigation of the penalties that left the real force of the Constitutions almost useless in obtaining the end desired. The cause of these delays was the doubt whether the *fiscus* of the Inquisition had to prove the existence of the evil purpose in those taking the Sacred Species, or whether the presumption of such purpose put the burden of proof on the accused. To settle this difficulty and to speed the trials and preclude the mitigation of penalties, Benedict XIV issued a constitution, *Ab Augustissimo,* March 5, 1744. After reënforcing the Constitutions of his predecessors, he declares: (1) After particles were taken or retained, the presumption was that they were consecrated. (2) The presumption that such taking or retaining the Sacred Species was for sacrilegious purposes was against the accused. To escape punishment, he must prove either that the particles were not consecrated, or, if they were, that he had a just cause for taking and retaining them. Unless this were clearly proved, all the afore-mentioned penalties were to be inflicted even for a first offense.[71]

Finally, Clement XIII, in the Constitution *Gravissimum* of March 6, 1759, makes it clear that the Constitutions of his predecessors were directed not only against the theft of the Holy Eucharist but also for any transfer, carrying away or retaining of It. Those who did any of these things were subject to trial and to the same penalties if they did not positively prove their purpose to be non-malicious. He then notes that even the former Constitutions, severe as they were, did not have the desired effect because the practice arose, in trying these cases, to deal leniently with those who spontaneously confessed their guilt. Sacrilegious men, abusing this mitigation, were thus undeterred from this great crime. Therefore, after confirming anew all the Constitutions of his predecessors, he declares the practice of the Holy Office of the Inquisition with regard to those who confess their guilt, no longer has any force, and that they are to be punished just as severely as those are who do not make this confession.[72]

The Code establishes, for the first time, a censure incurred

---

71. Fontes, n. 340

72. Fontes, n. 451; Petra, *op. cit.,* n. 9; Pignatelli, *Consultationes Canonicae,* cons. LXXXVI, Gasparri, *op. cit.,* II, p. 248.

ipso facto by those who cast away the Sacred Species or take them or retained them for a malicious purpose.[73] This censure is excommunication, the absolution from which is reserved in a most special way to the Holy See. Besides this, the one guilty of this crime is suspected of heresy, is *ipso facto* infamous and, if a cleric, he is to be deposed.

Though this penalty is incurred only by those who take or retain the Blessed Sacrament for an evil end, Canon 1265, §3, strictly forbids any private reservation of It. It also forbids the carrying of the Blessed Sacrament with one on a journey. The reason for this is found in the prohibition to carry It given the Italo-Greek monks by Benedict XIV: *Obsequium enim, ac reverentia, qua singuli fideles Augustissimum hoc Sacramentum prosequi debent, non patitur, ut privatim ac latenter, cuiuscumque arbitrio et voluntate, domi illud retineatur, aut in itineribus, ac peregrinationibus asportetur.*[74]

Similarly, an Encyclical Letter of the Sacred Congregation for the Propagation of the Faith calls the practice of missioners carrying the Blessed Sacrament about with them at all times, in order to administer It if they should meet a sick person, an abuse rather than a custom. It called to the minds of the Bishops that reverence due to this Sacrament, prompted the constant rigor of the Church in this matter and they are to see to it that the abuse is corrected as circumstances required and that the common practise of the Church be observed. The following decrees were also to be noted: S. C. S. Off. April 15, 1665, forbidding the missioners in China to carry the Blessed Sacrament with them on long journeys; and the Constitution of Benedict XIV, *Inter Omnigenas,* of February 2, 1744,[75] is quoted in regard to the rules to be followed in taking the Holy Viaticum to the sick by the priests in Serbia. The Holy Eucharist is not to be carried on a journey, except when taken to the sick and then it is to be done publicly, if possible, so that all due reverence may be given to It.[76]

This letter was also called to the mind of the missioners in the East Indies by the same Sacred Congregation in an in-

---

73. Canon 2320: Leech, *The Constitution Apostolicae Sedis and the Codex Juris Canonici,* p. 43.
74. *Etsi Pastoralis,* §VI. n. VII, *Fontes,* n. 328.
75. § 23, Fontes, n. 339.
76. Collectanea, n. 1171.

struction on September 8, 1869.[77] Another Instruction to the missioners among the Nestorians forbade them to give the Blessed Sacrament to the people at Easter time so that they might not miss Holy Communion if they should happen to be on a journey.[78]

The prohibition to carry the Blessed Sacrament with one on a journey is so strict, because It would not receive the reverence that is due to It. The one carrying It might be totally absorbed in meditation upon It, but the ignorance of the closeness of the Divine Presence, on the part of others, together with the consequent lack of respect which that Presence would evoke, is sufficient to forbid this exercise of piety. The Pope alone enjoys the privilege of carrying the Blessed Sacrament about with him.[79]

V. THE OPPORTUNITY FOR VISITING THE BLESSED SACRAMENT.

Churches where the Blessed Sacrament is reserved must be left open during some hours of the day so that the faithful may visit the Blessed Sacrament. The reason for this is plain. It would be entirely unbecoming that the faithful be prevented from visiting Jesus Christ present in the Holy Eucharist. The obligation to leave the church open for some hours daily is placed especially on parochial churches. But other churches in which the Blessed Sacrament is reserved are not exempt from this obligation. It is found also that it was required that oratories of Communities be left upon when the Blessed Sacrament was reserved in them in virtue of an Apostolic Indult. The Bishop of Bayonne, in a preamble to a question sent to the Sacred Congregation of Rites, says that one of the conditions on which an indult is given to oratories to reserve the Blessed Sacrament is that the door be open for some time each day. Nevertheless, the oratories of some Congregations of his diocese do not observe this because the condition is not placed in the rescript. Hence he asks: *An necesse omnino sit ut porta ad extra pateat? S. Rituum Congregatio ita rescribendum censuit: Negative in casu, attento Apostolico indulto.*[80]

77. Ibid., n. 1346.
78. Ibid., n. 2149.
79. Petra, *op. cit.*, n. 8.
80. Decr. Auth., n. 3706, ad III.

In a response sent to the Archbishop of Compostella, November 15, 1890, it was made an indispensable condition for the reservation of the Blessed Sacrament, that the doors of filial churches be left open for some time during the day.[81]

Today, though it is not a necessary condition for the reservation of the Blessed Sacrament, nevertheless it is the mind of the Church that the doors of the churches be left open so that the faithful may be free to enter and reverence their Sacramental Lord.

Where the Blessed Sacrament is reserved in the oratories of religious institutes of men, within their cloister, there is evidently no necessity for them having an outside door to admit the faithful in general. In fact, the law of the cloister for them excludes all women with the exception of these expressly given the privilege to enter by the Code.[82] Besides, it is sufficient that the community, for which the Blessed Sacrament is reserved, have ready approach to It. It is their duty to show this reverence, since it is for their benefit that It is reserved.

---

81. Decr. Auth., n. 3739, ad I; cf also Coll., n. 1742.
82. Canons 598, §1; 679, §2.

Canon 1268, §1. *Sanctissima Eucharistia continuo seu habitualiter custodiri nequit, nisi in uno tantum eiusdem ecclesiae altari.*

§2. *Custodiatur in praecellentissimo ac nobilissimo ecclesiae loco ac proinde regulariter in altari maiore, nisi aliud venerationi et cultui tanti sacramenti commodius et decentius videatur, servato praescripto legum liturgicarum quod ad ultimos dies hebdomadae maioris attinet.*

§3. *Sed in ecclesiis cathedralibus, collegiatis aut conventualibus in quibus ad altare maius chorales functiones persolvendae sunt, ne ecclesiasticis officiis impedimentum afferatur, opportunum est ut sanctissima Eucharistia regulariter non custodiatur in altri maiore, sed in alio sacello seu altari.*

§4. *Curent ecclesiarum rectores ut altare in quo sanctissimum Sacramentum asservatur sit prae omnibus aliis ornatum, ita ut suo ipso apparatu magis moveat fidelium pietatem ac devotionem.*

CHAPTER IV

THE ALTAR OF THE BLESSED SACRAMENT

UNTIL the publication of the *Roman Ritual* by Pope Paul V, in 1614, there was no general law requiring that the Blessed Sacrament should be kept on an altar.[1]

Among the practices in this regard, the more ancient was to keep the Blessed Sacrament, not in the church but in the *sacrarium*, a side room corresponding to what we know as the sacristy.[2]

Among the many evidences of this custom, it will suffice to give just one from the First Roman Ordo. In describing the ceremonies of the Pontifical Mass, it directed that the acolytes carry the Blessed Sacrament from the sacristy and show It to the Pontiff so that he might adore It on arriving at the altar.[3]

Though it was quite common to keep the Blessed Sacrament in the sacristy during those early days, nevertheless it was customary in some places to keep It in the church. Where this was done, the Blessed Sacrament was not ordinarily kept on the altar but in a dove-shaped vessel, called the *columbarium*, suspended over the altar.[4] This practice continued to be in use in some places as late as the nineteenth century.[5]

In the fourteenth and fifteenth centuries another method of reserving the Blessed Sacrament arose. It consisted in keeping

1. Braun, *Der Christliche Altar*, II, p. 591.
2. Ibid., p. 574.
3. *Ordo Rom. I*, n. 8; in Muratori, *Liturgia Romana Vetus*, II, 978-979; Corblet, *Histoire du Sacrement de L'Eucharistie*, II, p. 560; For further evidences of this custom of keeping the Blessed Sacrament in the sacristy the following sources may be consulted: *The Apostolic Constitutions*, lib. VIII, c. 13,—Migne, *P. G.*, I. 1110; Council of Macon, can. VI, Mansi, IX, 952; Council of Toledo (650), can. IV, Mansi, X, 777; Constitutiones Lateranenses, in Mabillon, *Museum Italicum*, II, p. 579; Martene, *De Ant. Eccl. Rit.*, l. I, c. III, p. 646; Mabillon, *In Ordinem Romanum Comm.*, in *Museum Italicum*, II, p. CXXXIX; Migne, *P. L.*, LXVVIII, 931; Smith-Cheetham, *Dictionary of Christian Antiquity*, II, 1565; Rock, *Hierurgia*, I, p. 267.
4. Braun, *op. cit.*, II, p. 574; Martingny, *Dictionnaire des Antiquites Chretiennes*, v. *Ciborium*, p. 188.
5. Braun, *loc. cit.*

the Blessed Sacrament in tower-like structures generally built on the walls of the choir, and which were called *Sakramentshäuschen*. Many of these can still be seen in the churches of Germany and the Netherlands, where this custom especially thrived.[6] The Synod of Brescia in the sixteenth century gave recognition to this custom in the following decree: *Tabernaculum vero vel ad cornu evangelii in pariete, more germanico, vel, quod mallemus, semper in summo altari, more romano, constituitur.*[7]

The Synod of Aquileia (1596) witnesses to another custom of keeping the Blessed Sacrament not in these towers but in recesses in the wall itself, when it forbids the hanging of pictures representing the Blessed Sacrament over them, lest the people be led to believe that It is there, whereas It is to be kept on the altar.[8] Nevertheless, through all these centuries, there are decrees of Councils requiring that the Blessed Sacrament should be kept on the altar of the church. The First Council of Tours (461) ordered that It be kept on the altar and protected from mice and evil men.[9] The second Council of Tours (567) decreed that the Body of the Lord was to be placed on the altar, and not among the images of the saints, but under the title of the cross—*non in imaginario ordine sed sub titulo crucis.*[10]

Martene relates how the effort to decide on the meaning of this canon has long tortured the genius of all those who have set about interpreting it. And in fact, there are many evidences of quite a controversy over the meaning of the canon. Among those that defended the position that the canon referred to the reservation of the Blessed Sacrament, are Mabillon,[11] Muratori,[12] Martene and others.[13]

Mabillon gives two other opinions on the meaning of this canon; the first that of a certain Sismond who maintained that it referred to the figure that was to be stamped on the host to be consecrated, requiring it to be a cross and not that of a saint;

6. Braun, *op. cit.*, II. p. 588.
7. Braun, *op. cit.*, *II*, pp. 591-593.
8. Ibid.
9. Can. IV, Mansi, VII, 950.
10. Can. III, Mansi, IX, 793.
11. *De Liturgia Gallicana*, 1. I, cap. IX, Migne, *P. L.*, LXXII, 164.
12. *Liturgia Romana Vetus*, I, 282.
13. *De Ant. Eccl. Rit.*, I, cap. V, art. III; Pignatelli, *Consultationes Canonicae*, tom. IV, cons. XXXI; Rohault de Fleury, *La Messe*, II, p. 58; Petra, *Comm. ad Const. I. Urbani IV*, n. 12.

the second, that the canon referred to the position of the chalice and the host at Mass, which were to be placed in the middle of the altar, *e regione crucis,* and not to the left or the right, *e regione imaginarium.* To these may be added another maintaining that the canon prescribes the arrangement of the pieces into which the host was to be broken at Mass. They were to be arranged in the form of a cross and not in any way that the individual imagination might suggest.[14]

The opinion of Mabillon and the others who agree with him is to be preferred for the reasons that he gives. The Blessed Sacrament was, according to this canon, to be kept on the altar under the cross because the words *imaginario ordine* mean nothing else than the order or place of the images and relics of the saint. It was in this sense that St. Athanasius used the words in his work on the Second Council of Nice, where he speaks of the *pictura imaginaria,* and in his work against Elipandus, where he uses the term *imaginarie,* i. e., according to an image. Secondly, the words *titulus crucis* in those early days were often taken to mean the cross itself, an example of which is found in the work of an anonymous monk on *The Miracles of St. Bercharius.* Writing of the death of a certain Hugo, he says: *In titulo crucis, qui stabat ad pedes artificis etc.,* meaning only the cross. Finally, relics were very rarely, if ever, kept on the altar. They were usually placed in recesses in the wall or in the sacristy. The Blessed Sacrament was, therefore, in virtue of this canon of the Council of Tours, to be reserved not among these, but under the cross which was suspended over the altar from the baldachin.[15]

The foundation for the opinion of Dr. Rock is the vision of a certain Spanish Bishop, Ildephonsus. But from a glance at the account of this vision and the accompanying illustration in the *Patrologia Latina* of Migne, it can be seen that there is question of many particles and not of the breaking of one large host.[16] Furthermore, the First Roman Ordo prescribed that the Host at Mass was to be broken into only three pieces, one of

---

14. Rock, *The Church of Our Fathers,* I, p. 92.

15. Mabillon, *De Azymo et Fermentato,* in Cienfuegos, *Bibliotheca de Azymo,* cap. VIII, pp. 58 sqq.; Muratori, *Liturgia Romana Vetus,* I, 282.

16. Migne, *P. L.,* CVI, 883.

which was to be dropped into the chalice, thus making it impossible to arrange the parts of the Host in the form of a cross.[17]

Another evidence of the spread of the custom that reserved the Blessed Sacrament on the altar is to be found in the Second Roman Ordo, where the Blessed Sacrament is no longer carried from the sacristy but is already on the altar when the Pontiff arrives there.[18] Again, evidence of this is found in the decree of Bishop Ratherius of Verona in his *Synodica* (966), repeating an earlier *Admonitio Synodalis* on this point: *Super altare nihil aliud ponatur nisi capsae, et quatuor Evangelia et pyxis cum corpore Domini ad viaticum infirmis; cetera nitido loco recondatur.*[19] From this time on the practice spread very rapidly throughout the Church but it was always in virtue of the particular legislation of various provincial councils or the regulations of the bishops for their dioceses.[20]

At the end of the Middle Ages, there was still no general written legislation requiring that the Blessed Sacrament should be kept on the altar. The *Caeremoniale Episcoporum*, published by Pope Clement VIII, did not make it obligatory to keep the Blessed Sacrament on an altar, but speaks of this as being the ordinary practice. *Nam licet sacrosancto Domini nostri Jesu Christi omnium Sacramentorum fonti, praecellentissimus ac nobilissimus omnium locus in ecclesia conveniat, neque humanis viribus illud venerari et colere umquam valeamus, quantum debet, tenemurque; tamen valde opportunum est, illud non collocetur in maiori, vel in alio altari, in quo episcopus vel alius solemniter est Missam, seu Vesperas celebraturus: sed in alio sacello, seu loco ornatissimo cum omni decentia, et reverentia ponatur.*[21]

From this quotation one can only conclude that an altar was the most becoming place to reserve the Blessed Sacrament but that, where the main altar is not to be used in the circum-

---

17. *Ordo Rom. I*, nn. 19 & 22, in Mabillon, *Museum Italicum, Ant. Lib. Rit.*, pp. 13 & 16.

18. *Ordo Rom. II*, n. 4, in Muratori, *Liturgia Romana Vetus*, II, 1020; Migne, *P. L.*, LXXVIII, 931; Martene, *De Ant. Eccl. Rit.*, p. 647; *Homilia Leonis IV*, in Mansi, XIV, 891.

19. Migne, *P. L.*, CXV, 677; CXXXVI, 559; Mansi, XVIIIA, 369.

20. *Synodal Constitutions* fo Odo, Bishop of Paris (1197), nn. 1 & 6, Mansi, XXII, 678; Oxon., Mansi, XXII, 1175; Conc. Mediol. I, Acta Eccl. Mediol., pars I, p. 8; *Instructio de SS. Euch.*, pars IV, p. 513; *Instr. Fabr. Eccl.*, l. I, in Acta, pars IV, p. 568.

21. Caer. Episcoporum, l. I, cap. XII, n. 8.

stances mentioned, it did not command that It be kept on another altar. All that it stated was that the Blessed Sacrament be reserved in another place appropriately adorned.[22]

The first general legislation that required the Blessed Sacrament should be reserved on an altar is found in the *Rituale Romanum* (1614): *Tabernaculum. . . .in altare maiori vel in alio. . . .sit collocatum.*[23] From that time on, though there is no further decree that repeated this prescription of the Ritual, there are many that solve doubts in a way that presupposes the Blessed Sacrament is kept only on the altar of the church concerned.

It may be kept on one altar of a church or oratory. The practice of reserving It on more than oe altar was forbidden in a decree of the Sacred Congregation of Rites on March 14, 1861. Asked, *Utrum ferri possit consuetudo plurium ecclesiarum Archidioeceseos N. et praesertim Regularium, asservandi Sanctissimam Eucharistiam in duobus vel tribus altaribus; et nonnumquam occasione novemdialis aut alicuius festivitatis transferendi etiam in aliud altare diversum ab illis, in quibus ordinarie asservatur?*, the response was: *Negative.*[24]

A multiplicity of reasons for reserving the Blessed Sacrament in one church does not permit that It be kept on more than one altar. These reasons may arise, for instance, in a church that is a cathedral or belongs to an Order and is at the same time parochial in its functions. The Blessed Sacrament may not be kept on one altar because the church is a cathedral or belongs to Regulars and on another altar because it is parochial.[25] The Code is very clear on this point. The Blessed Sacrament may not be kept habitually on more than one altar of the church. And as a church is a sacred building dedicated to divine worship, the Blessed Sacrament may not be kept in the basement of the church and in the body of the church at the same time. The basement is an integral part of the building.[26]

As Canon 1268, §1, forbids only the habitual reservation of the Blessed Sacrament on more than one altar, it is permissible to keep It on a second altar on some special occasion or to facili-

22. Braun, *op. cit.*, II, p. 591.
23. Tit. IV, c. 1, *dt sanctissimo Eucharistiae sacramento*, n. 6.
24. Decr. Auth., n. 3104, ad XIII.
25. S. R. C., July 21, 1696, ad III, Decr. Auth., n. 1946.
26. Canon 1161; cf. Canon 1164 §2 where it is forbidden to use the basement of the church for profane uses, indicating that it is a part of the sacred building mentioned in Canon 1161.

tate the distribution of Holy Communion. It is to be left on this second altar only for the time that is necessary to satisfy these purposes.[27]

There is only one exception for the habitual reservation of the Blessed Sacrament on more than one altar and that is in churches where there is perpetual exposition of It or during the Forty Hours devotion. This arises from the prohibition to say Mass or to distribute Holy Communion from an altar where the Blessed Sacrament is exposed, unless there is a grave reason or an indult has been obtained for a contrary procedure.[28]

Immediately after the Sacred Congregation forbade the saying of Mass or the distributing of Holy Communion at an altar where the Blessed Sacrament is exposed, it issued another decree requiring that It be kept on an altar other than the altar of Exposition, for the distribution of Holy Communion.[29] For the same reason the Blessed Sacrament is to be kept on a side altar when there is exposition of It on the main altar during the Forty Hours devotion.[30]

The altar to be used for the reservation of the Blessed Sacrament is the main altar as being generally the most fitted and elegant. However, if there is another altar that is more beautiful and better fitted to inspire reverence for the Holy Eucharist and to facilitate the approach of the worshippers, it is to be chosen. This canon requires merely that the best altar be given over to this purpose and as a rule this will be the main altar.[31] But since the main altar need not be chosen as the one for the Blessed Sacrament, it is not necessary to construct it with this purpose in view. Another altar may be selected and constructed for this along the lines laid down by the Bishop.[32]

Though the Blessed Sacrament will be kept on the main altar, generally, as the one most becoming, nevertheless, this does not forbid the transfer of It to another altar during a triduum,

---

27. Vermeersch-Creusen, *Epitome*, II, p. 344; Fanfani, *De Jure Religiosorum*, p. 415.

28. S. R. C., May 11, 1878, ad I, Decr. Auth., n. 3448. This response was referred to by the Sacred Congregation of Rites again on April 17, 1919, A. A. S., XI, p. 246.

29. S. R. C., May 18, 1878, ad III, Decr. Auth., n. 3449.

30. S. R. C., Nov. 23, 1880, ad IV, Decr. Auth., n. 3525.

31. Petra, *op. cit.*, n. 16; Catalanus, *Comm. in Caer. Epp.*, l. I. cap. XII, §VIII, p. 242; Gasparri, *op. cit.*, II, p. 259; Cappello, *De Sacramentis*, I, p. 259.

32. S. R. C., May 18, 1878, ad I & II, Decr. Auth., n. 3449.

novena or other exercises on the occasion of the feast day of some saint. This may be done provided the Blessed Sacrament is not kept on two altars in the church at the same time.[33]

In designating the altar for the reservation of the Blessed Sacrament in cathedral, collegiate and conventual churches, the Code uses practically the same words as the *Caeremoniale Episcoporum*.[34] It declares that on account of the choral functions, it is opportune that the Blessed Sacrament be kept on altar other than the main altar or in another chapel. On the face of it, this does not seem to be anything more than a recommendation that the main altar be not used in these churches. But before the Code, the replies of the Sacred Congregations to questions on this point made it a prohibition to keep the Blessed Sacrament on the main altar.[35] For cathedral churches, the Sacred Congregation of Bishops and Regulars declared: *Tabernaculum Sanctissimi Sacramenti in cathedralibus non debet esse in altari maiori propter functiones pontificales quae fiunt versis renibus ad altare.*[36]

And the Sacred Congregation of Rites declared against a century old custom of reserving the Blessed Sacrament on the main altar of a cathedral, because of its peculiar structure: *An, attenta peculiari structura ecclesiae cathedralis N. et saeculari consuetudine in eadem vigente, retineri possit Sanctissimum Eucharistiae Sacramentum in altari maiori; eo vel magis quod id non vetetur a Caeremoniali Episcoporum, sed solum uti minus opportunum perhibeatur? Responsio fuit: Negative.*[37] The form of this latter question, in proposing as an excuse for the custom, the fact that the *Caeremoniale Episcoporum* made it only opportune that the Blessed Sacrament be not kept on the main altar of the cathedral, and the negative response to the request for the toleration of the custom to keep It there, make it clear that there was a strict prohibition contained in the words of the *Caeremoniale Episcoporum* as interpreted by the Sacred

---

33. S. R. C., June 2, 1883, ad VI, Decr. Auth., n. 3576; Pignatelli, *Consultationes Canonicae*, I. cons. XXXI; Gasparri, *op. cit.*, II, p. 260; Van der Stappen, *Sacra Liturgia*, IV, p. 102; Cappello, *De* 260; Van der Stappen, *Sacra Liturgia*, IV, p. 102; Cappello, *De Sacramentis*, I, p. 260.
34. Lib. I, cap. XII, n. VIII.
35. Vermeersch-Creusen, *Epitome*, II, p. 345; Cappello, *De Sacramentis*, I, p. 263.
36. Petra, *op. cit.*, n. 16.
37. Feb. 6, 1875, ad I, Decr. Auth., n. 3335; Apr. 26, 1901, ad III, ibid. n., 4071.

the Code and its restatement there without any substantial change, it seems that the prohibition of the older law for cathedrals, at least, still is in force.[38]

The reason given for not reserving the Blessed Sacrament on the main altar in these churches is that of the choir functions. When these are solemnly celebrated before the altar of the Blessed Sacrament, the number of the genuflections is increased and interferes with the ordinary rubrics for these ceremonies. It was the custom in some collegiate and conventual churches to transfer the Blessed Sacrament to another altar during the Solemn High Mass, but where such Masses are celebrated very frequently, it is better to keep the Blessed Sacrament on another altar all the time in order to avoid any irreverence that might arise from the frequent transfer of It from one altar to another.[39]

In cathedral churches there is the additional reason that many of the pontifical functions are celebrated by the Bishop with his back to the altar. It is certainly unbecoming that this altar should be used for the reservation of the Blessed Sacrament. And when the Bishop pontificates in other churches, the Blessed Sacrament should be removed from the altar for the same reason.[40] As far as possible the altar of the Blessed Sacrament should not be one that is in the sight of the choir, so that their functions may not be interrupted by the removal of the Blessed Sacrament from the tabernacle either for the purpose of giving Holy Communion or of taking It to the sick.[41]

The altar of the Blessed Sacrament is to be the most beautifully adorned of all the altars of the church and it is for the rector of the church to see to this. The reason for this is plain. Since our Lord is present on the altar, Body and Blood, Soul and Divinity, it is not only becoming but also obligatory that the greatest care be taken that the altar on which He abides should be of more precious material and more beautifully ornamented than any other altar in the church. The worship that can and should be given by such care is none other than that of absolute adoration. External appreciation and devotion to the Congregation. In virtue of this interpretation of the law before

38. Canon 6, n. 2.

39. Petra, *op. cit.*, n. 17; Gasparri, *op. cit.*, II, p. 260.

40. Caer. Epp. 1. I, cap. XII, n. VIII; Pignatelli, *Consultationes Canonicae*, I, cons. XXXI; Cappello, *op. cit.*, I, pp. 263-264.

41. S. R. C., June 14, 1845, Decr. Auth., n. 2903; Cappello, *loc cit.*

Blessed Sacrament should be greater than that to any of the saints as well as interior appreciation and devotion. Hence when there is question of adorning altars with flowers, lights and such, the altar of the Blessed Sacrament should always be favored. In no other way can it be better kept before the minds of the people that the center of devotion in the church is the Blessed Sacrament, than by having Its altar conspicuous and outstanding for its beauty.[42]

Formerly, a baldachin was to be built over the altar of the Blessed Sacrament as well as over every altar where Mass was celebrated. There are two decrees of the Sacred Congregation of Rites requiring this. Asked whether the baldachin was to be erected over the altar of the Blessed Sacrament only, or over all the altars, it replied that it was to be erected over all altars.[43] However, in the reference to these decrees in the index to the *Decreta Authentica,* there is a parenthetical note to the effect that even at Rome their observance has fallen into desuetude. They were never generally observed outside of Italy.[44] Among the questions to be answered in the report on the Apostolic Visitation of Rome and its district, Pope Pius X included one on whether or not there was a balachin over the altars of the Blessed Sacrament.[45]

The decoration of the altar of the Blessed Sacrament should be such as to excite the devotion of the people. The lines along which this is to be done have been laid down by the Sacred Congregation of Rites in various decrees. Nothing productive of a theatrical effect is permitted in the adornment of the altar. Specifically, neither gas nor electric lights are to be placed on the altar.[46] This prohibition of anything theatrical in the decoration of the altar of the Blessed Sacrament includes also spot lights focussed on the tabernacle. A stronger reason for the prohibition of such lights is found in the decree allowing the use

---

42. Cappello, *op. cit.* I, p. 264; Vermeersch-Creusen, *Epitome,* II, p. 345.

43. Apr. 27, 1697, Decr. Auth., n. 1966; May 23, 1846, ibid. n. 2912.

44. Corblet, *Histoire du Sacrement de L' Eucharistie.* I, p. 573; Van der Stappen, *Sacra Liturgia,* IV, p. 123.

45. A. S. S., XXXVII, p. 204; Van der Stappen, *op. cit.,* IV, p. 123.

46. S. R. C., Nov. 29, 1901, Decr. Auth., n. 4086; May 16, 1902, *ibid.,* n. 4097; Nov. 22, 1907, *ibid.,* n. 4206.

of gas or electric lights in the church only for the purpose of illumination and forbidding them as part of the worship.[47]

In the adornment of the altar of the Blessed Sacrament, it is allowed to place a statue of our Lord in which His Sacred Heart is prominent, behind the tabernacle, but in no way is it allowed to place it on the tabernacle.[48]

Finally, in regard to the proper respect due to the altar where the Blessed Sacrament is reserved, it may be noted, that in institutions where the oratory, in which It is reserved, is built into the house, it is forbidden to use the rooms above the altar for living rooms and much less for sleeping rooms. The Sacred Congregation of Rites was asked: *Utrum liceat asservare Sanctissimam Eucharistiam in altari baldachinum habente, quamvis super illud habeatur habitaculum cum lectulo?* The answer was, *Negative ex decreto* 3525, *ad II.*[49]

The decree, here referred to, gave to the Daughters of Charity, called Canossians, the privilege to use the rooms above the altar of the Blessed Sacrament for a dormitory, provided a baldachin was built over the altar.[50] This indult was granted to them because of the grave inconvenience and the loss that would be suffered in arranging other places for the dormitory. The general law is firmly against such a practice and in constructing these institutions arrangements should be made beforehand to provide that no living rooms will be above the altar of the Blessed Sacrament if the oratory is built into the house.[51]

The rector of the church or oratory is directly responsible for the proper care of the altar of the Blessed Sacrament. The term "rector" is not to be taken here in the strict sense of Canon 479, §1. There it is limited to the priest in charge of a church that is neither parochial, capitular, nor attached to the house of religious community. And in such churches, the Blessed Sacrament is not generally reserved. The term is, therefore, used in this canon (1268, §4) to comprehend every priest who has the charge of a church or oratory where the Blessed Sacrament is reserved. It includes then, the pastor, chaplain, chapters and

---

47. S. R. C., June 4, 1895, Decr. Auth., n. 3859
48. S. R. C., April 23, 1926, A. A. S., XVIII, p. 291.
49. Jan. 24, 1908, ad III, Decr. Auth., n. 4213.
50. S. R. C., Nov. 23, 1880, ad II, Decr. Auth., n. 3525.
51. Van der Stappen, *Sacra Liturgia*, IV, pp. 122-123.

religious communities.[52] It is their privilege and duty to see that the altar of the Blessed Sacrament is given special attention in its beautification over that of all the other altars of the church, and in this way to increase the devotion of the faithful to this great Sacrament.

52. Canons 415, §3, n. 1; 609, §1; Rituale Rom., tit. IV, cap. 1, *de sanctissimo Eucharistiae sacramento,* n. 2; Blat, *Comm. Text. C. I. C.* lib. III, pars III, p. 165.

Canon 1269. §1. *Sanctissima Eucharistia servari debet in tabernaculo inamovibili in media parte altaris posito.*

§2. *Tabernaculum sit affabre exstructum, undequaque solide clausum, decenter ornatum ad norman legum liturgicarum, ab omni alia re vacuum, ac tam sedulo custodiatur ut periculum cuiusvis sacrilegae profanationis arceatur.*

§3. *Gravi aliqua suadente causa ab Ordinario loci probata, non est vetitum sanctissimam Eucharistiam nocturno tempore extra altare, super corporali tamen, in loco tutiore et decenti, asservari, servato, praescripto can.* 1271.

§4. *Clavis tabernaculi, in quo sanctissimum Sacramentum asservatur, diligentissime custodiri debet, onerata graviter conscientia sacerdotis qui ecclesiae vel oratorii curam habet.*

CHAPTER V.

THE TABERNACLE

IN the absence of any general legislation requiring the reservation of the Blessed Sacrament on an altar until the publication of the Roman Ritual in 1614, there was no legislation of this kind that referred to the tabernacle.

As was noted before, the most common of the early methods of reserving the Blessed Sacrament was to suspend the sacred vessels in which It was kept, over the altar. The Blessed Sacrament was also kept in recesses in the wall, in tower-like receptacles standing at the right or left of the altar, and in the Sacrament Houses built on the walls of the choir. Whichever of these different methods was used, the Blessed Sacrament was reserved in it to serve specifically as Viaticum for the dying. The other faithful who might wish to receive Holy Communion were comunicated with Particles consecrated at the Mass they attended.[1]

Tabernacles resembling more or less those in use today originated about the thirteenth century. Their origin is found in the wooden or metal caskets in which the pyx was kept about this time. They were usually covered with a silk canopy and placed on the right or left side of the altar as well as in the middle of it.[2]

The necessity for tabernacles arose from the decrees of Popes Innocent III and Honorius III, requiring that the Blessed Sacrament must be kept locked in a place for It alone.[3] To comply with these regulations, some sort of container for the pyx holding the Blessed Sacrament was necessary. The pyx could be adequately protected or safeguarded from the dangers of irreverence, which these decrees intended to prevent, only by

1. Corblet, *Histoire du Sacrement de L'Eucharistie*, I. p. 560; II, p. 287; Rohault de Fleury, *La Messe*, II, pp. 57-58; Braun, *Der Christliche Altar*, I. pp. 574. 582-583.

2. Corblet, *op. cit.*, I, p. 561.

3. C. 1, X, *de custodia Eucharistiae, chrismatis, et aliorum sacramentorum*, III, 44; c. 10, X, *de celebratione missarum, et sacramento Eucharistiae, et divinis officiis*, III, 41.

inclosing it in a kind of box or casket. When it became obligatory to keep the Blessed Sacrament on the altar, the construction of tabernacles to provide a suitable place for It, became necessary. However, as late as the seventeenth century, there are evidences that the tabernacle in some dioceses was suspended from the baldachin over the altar.[4]

The tabernacle at present must be built in the center of the altar. It is also to be built into the altar so as to avoid the possibility of it being wantonly carried away or accidentally toppled over. There is one exception to this rule of the tabernacle being on the altar, in virtue of an indult granted to the Coletines in the Archdiocese of Cambrai. They are allowed to keep the Blessed Sacrament in a small opening in the wall between the sanctuary and their choir.[5] Elsewhere it is forbidden to revert to the ancient practices of keeping the Blessed Sacrament in Eucharistic towers, dove-shaped vessels or the like, though these practices may have been in use formerly in some particular churches.[6]

But where these customs may have been continuous, they need not be abolished if they are immemorial or a century old and if the Bishop allows them. They have not been reprobated by the Code. If the practice is of shorter duration, they are revoked because the Code gives them no recognition.[7]

Some maintain that none of these customs may be continued. The reason they give is based on a letter written to the Bishop of Limburg by the Sacred Congregation of Rites in the name of Pius IX on August 21, 1863. Besides the fact that this letter is of a strictly private character and is not found in the official collection of the Acts of the Sacred Congregation, there is the added reason against its force as an argument for the abolition of all uninterrupted customs, because it was written to prevent the movement in some places to resume the older methods of reserving the Blessed Sacrament. It expressly forbade changes that would revive these methods in older churches or to introduce them into new churches. Between this and the pro-

4. S. R. C., June 10, 1602, ad V; Nov. 22. 1659; Decr. Auth., nn. 96, 1132; Rohault de Fleury, *La Messe*, II, pp. 69 sqq.

5. S. R. C., Dec. 11, 1885, ad I, Decr. Auth., n. 3648; Van der Stappen, *Sacra Liturgia*, IV, pp. 110-111.

6. Gasparri, *op. cit*, II, p. 263; Van der Stappen, *op. cit.*, IV, p. 110.

7. Canon 5; Woywod, "Law of the Code on the Divine Cult," art. *Tabernacle*, in *The Homiletic and Pastoral Review*, vol. XXVII, p. 150.

hibition of a custom that never was discontinued, there is a distinct and unmistakable difference.[8]

The position of the tabernacle on the altar should not be such as to inconvenience a priest saying Mass there. It should not be so near the front of the altar as not to give him sufficient room for the Chalice and Host at Mass, nor so far back that a riser is necessary in order for him to remove the pyx for the distribution of Holy Communion.[9]

The material of the tabernacle is not determined by any general law of the Church. According to a declaration of the Sacred Congregation of Bishops and Regulars, it should ordinarily be of wood gilded on the outside.[10]

But the tabernacle may also be made of stone or precious metals as St. Charles Borromeo recommended in churches with the resources to do so, in order that as much reverence as possible might be shown the Blessed Sacrament.[11] Where the tabernacle is not made of wood, it is fitting that it be lined with it in order that there may be as little dampness as possible in the tabernacle and thus lessen the danger of rapid corruption of the Hosts.[12]

The tabernacle is to be solidly built and closed on all sides. This is necessary in order that all danger of anything happening to the Sacred Species from climate, insects or other natural causes, as well as to prevent thefts of the ciborium. It is forbidden to construct the tabernacle or to include in its construction any materials that permit the pyx to be seen.[13] It is desirable also that the tabernacle should be made as nearly fire-proof as possible. This can be accomplished to some extent by the application of present-day methods in making safes. In recent years a tabernacle has been designed that is as nearly burglar and fire-proof as possible. Instead of the door swinging on hinges, those of the newer models slide back on rollers on the turning of the key. The approval of these tabernacles is left to the

8. Gasparri, *loc. cit.;* Van der Stappen, *loc. cit.;* Cappello, *De Sacramentis,* I, p. 265.

9. Acta Eccl. Mediol. (*Decrata Visitatoris Apostolici*), pars III, p. 464; Van der Stappen, *op. cit.*, IV, p. 113

10. De Herdt, *Sacrae Liturgiae Praxis,* III, n. 180; Woywod, *art. cit.; also* cf. S. R. C., Dec. 7, 1888, ad XIII, Decr. Auth., n. 3697.

11. *Instr. Fabricae Eccl.* 1. I, in Acta Eccl. Mediol, pars, IV, p. 568.

12. Ibid.

13. S. R. C., Sept. 20, 1806, ad II, Decr. Auth., n. 2564.

Bishops by the Sacred Congregation of Rites, which honored the designers with a letter of commendation.[14]

In some churches there are tabernacles with a door in the rear as well as the one opening to the front. These serve a very useful purpose in enabling a priest to get the Blessed Sacrament for a sick call during Mass without disturbing the celebrant. As long as these doors do not make the custody of the Blessed Sacrament less secure, there is nothing that forbids them. In fact, St. Charles Borromeo recommended such a door, especially in the larger churches where the choir was behind the altar, in order that Communion might be given them more easily.[15]

There is no special form required for the tabernacle. It may be round or square or any form acording to the design of the altar.[16]

A representation of the Sacred Heart is not to be placed on the main altar instead of the tabernacle.[17]

All that is allowed on the top of the tabernacle is a small cross.[18]

Images or relics of the saints or flowers may not be placed on the tabernacle in such a way that the tabernacle serves as the pedestal for them.[19]

Neither may any of these or other things be placed before the door of the tabernacle.[20]

Before the door of the tabernacle it is only allowed to place the altar cards and they may be left there only during the time of Mass.[21]

The tabernacle is to be covered with a canopy as the Ritual prescribes.[22]

However beautiful or precious the tabernacle itself may be, the canopy is to be used.[23]

The use of the veil on the interior of the tabernacle or

---

14. *Ephemerides Liturgicae*, XXII, pp. 204-206: Cappello, *De Sacramentis*, I, p. 265.
15. *Instr. Fabr. Eccl.*, 1. I, in Acta Eccl. Mediol., pars IV, p. 568
16. Ibid.
17. S. R. C., May 31, 1887, ad II, Decr. Auth., n. 3673
18. S. R. C., June 16, 1663, ad I; Mar. 12, 1836, ad I, Decr. Auth., nn. 1270, 2740.
19. S. R. C., Apr. 3, 1821, ad IV, Decr. Auth., n. 2613.
20. S. R. C., Jan. 22, 1701, ad X; Sept. 6, 1845; Sept. 10, 1898, ad I; June 11, 1904, ad I; Decr. Auth., nn. 2067, 2906, 4000, 4136.
21. S. R. C., Aug. 4, 1905, ad II, Decr. Auth., n. 4165.
22. Tit. IV, cap. 1, *de sanctissimo Eucharistiae sacramento* n. 16.
23. S. R. C., Aug. 7, 1880, Decr. Auth., n. 3520.

hanging inside over the opening of it cannot be considered as supplying the use of the canopy, nor can the custom of not having the canopy be given as a just reason for its absence. A very clear response on this point is found in the answer given to the following question: *An servari possit consuetudo non adhibendi canopaeum quo tegi debet tabernaculum ubi asservatur Sanctissimum Eucharistiae Sacramentum?* The reply was: *Negative, et servetur Rituale Romanum et decreta.*[24]

A valid reason for not using the canopy may be found in the impossibility of being able to use one on the tabernacle becomingly. If the canopy cannot be artistically arranged on the tabernacle, because of its form, it is better and more fitting that it be not used. This is the case with many of the tabernacles in our country.[25]

Moreover, where the use of the canopy may be the cause of danger to the Blessed Sacrament, its use may be dispensed with. Thus the Holy See leaves it to the prudence of the Ordinaris in the tropics to have the tabernacle covered with the canopy or to dispense with it, because of the fact that insects in those regions nest in it and from it find their way into the tabernacle.[26]

The material of the canopy may be hemp, cotton, wool, silk or silver or gold cloth.[27]

As regards the colors of the canopy, white may be used all the time or the color may be changed to correspond with the color of the vestments each day, or the season of the year. But on All Souls' Day and at funeral and Requiem High Masses, the color of the canopy is to be purple. It is never allowed to use a black canopy.[28]

The interior of the tabernacle is to be covered with a silk lining, with gold or silver plate or at least gilded.[29]

The floor of the tabernacle is to be covered with a corporal, to be changed as often as neatness and cleanliness require.

---

24. July 1, 1904, Decr. Auth., n. 4137; cf also Apr. 28, 1866, Decr. Auth., n. 3150.

25. Woywod, *art. cit.*

26. S. R. C., July 27, 1878, Decr. Auth., n. 3456.

27. S. R. C., July 21, 1855, ad X, Decr. Auth., n. 3035.

28. S. R. C., July 21, 1855, ad X: Dec. 1, 1882, Decr. Auth., nn. 3035, 3562.

29. S. R. C., June 5, 1889; June 20, 1899; Aug. 7, 1871, ad VII, Decr. Auth. nn. 3709, 4035, 3254.

This obligation for the Church in general is one of custom, as there is no written law requiring it. In our country it is obligatory also from a decree of the Second Plenary Council of Baltimore.[30]

Inside the tabernacle nothing is to be kept except the pyx containing the Blessed Sacrament. An empty pyx that has not been purified may also be kept there. It is not allowed to keep the other sacred vessels, the holy oils, relics or anything else, in the tabernacle.[31]

It is also forbidden to put an electric light in the interior of the tabernacle, so that the Blessed Sacrament may be better seen in private or public exposition.[32]

Finally, the tabernacle is to be blessed. Whatever the older authors said about obligation in this matter, the obligation is made clear by the following response of the Sacred Congregation of Rites. The question asked was: *Utrum sacrum tabernaculum. . . .sit benedicenum, priusquam Sacra Eucharistia in illo recondatur?* The answer was: *Affirmative.*[33]

The formula to be used for this blessing is that in the Ritual entitled *Benedictio Tabernaculi seu Vasculi.*[34] This blessing can be given by Cardinals, Bishops and those local Ordinaries that have not the episcopal character, for the churches and oratories of their territory, the pastor for the parish church and the oratories in the parish, rectors of churches for their own churches only, priests delegated by the local Ordinary within the limits of the delegation and the territory of the one delegating them, and religious Superiors and their delegates for their own churches and those of the nuns who may be subject to them.[35]

If, in spite of all the precautions taken to make the tabernacle secure, there remains the danger of sacrilegious theft of the Holy Eucharist, or for any other just cause, the local Ordinary may allow It to be kept in a safe during the night. When this

30. Conc. Balt. II, tit. V, n. 266; Pignatelli, *Consultationes Canonicae*, tom. IX, p. 25; Cappello, *op. cit.*, I, p. 276.

31. Rit. Rom., tit. IV, cap. 1, *de sanctissimo Eucharistiae sacramento*, n. 6; S. C. Epp. et Reg., 3 Maii 1693, in Cavalieri, *Rituale Expensum*, p. 230; Gasparri, *op. cit.*, II, p. 265; Cappello, *op. cit.*, I, p. 268.

32. S. R. C., July 28, 1911, A. A. S., III, p. 396; Decr. Auth., n. 4275.

33. June 20, 1899, ad IV, Decr. Auth., n. 4035.

34. Tit. VIII, cap. 23.

35. Canon 1304.

is done, the pyx must be placed on a corporal and a light must be kept burning before It. The Ordinary may also allow the pastor to keep the Blessed Sacrament in his own house when the church is some distance away, in order that sick calls may be attended to as promptly as possible.[36] It is not necessary that there be anyone actually sick in the parish in order that this permission be given. Moreover, in places where Catholics use the same building for worship as non-Catholics, the Blessed Sacrament must be kept in the pastor's house.[37]

One of the essential elements in the diligent custody of the Blessed Sacrament is that the tabernacle be securely locked. As was said before, the use of the tabernacle began to spread rapidly on the promulgation of the following decree of Pope Innocent III in the Fourth Lateran Council. *Statuimus, ut in cunctis ecclesiis chrisma et Eucharistia sub fideli custodia clavibus adhibitis conserventur, ne possit ad illa temeraria manus extendi ad aliqua horribilia vel nefaria exercenda. Si vero is, ad quem spectat custodia, ea incaute dereliquerit, tribus mensibus ab officio suspendatur, et, si per eius incuriam aliquid nefandum inde contigerit, graviori subiaceat ultioni.*[38]

This was the first time that the Church required that the tabernacle be kept locked.

The custody of the tabernacle key belonged to the pastor or chaplain of the church or oratory to the exclusion of everyone else. Thus the Sacred Congregation of the Council decided in the answer it made to the following question: *An clavis tabernaculi stare debeat penes archipresbyterum aut penes capellanos confratres?* The reply was: *Penes Archipresbyterum privative.*[39]

Similarly, in another response on November 14, 1693: *An claves sacri tabernaculi retinendae sint a solo parocho privative ad sacristam a confraternitate deputatum, an vero liceat sacristae aliam clavem retinere?* The answer was: *Affirmative pro parocho.*[40]

In regard to the key of the tabernacle in the chapels of

---

36. S. R. C., Feb. 4, 1871, ad I, n. 5, Decr. Auth., n. 3234.

37. S. C. de Prop. Fide, Mar. 7, 1805, Coll. n. 681.

38. C. I. X, *de custodia Eucharistiae, chrismatis et aliorum sacramentorum*, III, 44.

39. S. C. C. *in Ausculana*, 25 Junii, 1689, in, Petra: *op. cit.* n. 41 Pignatelli, *op. cit.* tom. VI, cons. LXXXVII, p. 205.

40. Petra, *ibid;* Gasparri, *op. cit.* II, p. 266.

nuns, the chaplain was to keep it and it was not to be kept within the cloister. *Invaluit usus apud moniales ut clavis tabernaculi non penes cappellanum sed inter septa monasterii asservetur, etiam cum domus cappellani finitima est monasterio, Anne servari potest talis usus? Et S. R. C. respondendum censuit Negative.*[41] For a still greater reason therefore the key could not *be kept by laics.*[42]

The Holy See has always been most strict in requiring that the key to the tabernacle be kept by the priest in charge of the Blessed Sacrament. And the priest was to keep the key where it could not be reached by anyone else. The Sacred Congregation of Bishops and Regulars, March 25, 1591, severely rebuked a pastor who left the tabernacle key where it could be easily taken without his knowledge. Another priest had given Holy Communion to a person in the parochial church without having asked the pastor for the key. The Bishop was told to look into the carelessness of the pastor in thus leaving the key about and was to punish him severely and without mitigation if it should happen again.[43] This was in line with the declaration of Innocent III that penalties were to be inflicted even if no sacrileges followed from such carelessness.

An even more severe letter was sent out by the same Sacred Congregation on February 9, 1751. The occasion of this letter was the increase in criminal and sacrilegious thefts of the Holy Eucharist due to the malice of men and the carelessness of those who had the duty of guarding the Blessed Sacrament. Every Ordinary in his diocese, territory or district was to enjoin and inculcate in most urgent and efficacious terms that parish priests, rectors, sacristans or others who have charge of the tabernacles, not to be wanting in the most jealous care and to keep the keys personally or to put them in a safe place under another key, in such a way that the sacred vessels of the Holy Eucharist may never be exposed to the danger of being violated or touched. If by negligence, forgetfulness or any other culpable ommission of those who are the custodians of the Blessed Sacrament a sacrilegious theft should take place without a violent breaking of the tabernacle, and particularly if it had been left open or the

41. Decr. Auth., n. 3448 ad VI: cf. also S. C. Epp. et Reg. March 12, 1705, Fontes, n. 1822: Gasparri, *loc. cit.*
42. Petra, *loc. cit.*
43. Fontes, n. 1442.

keys left in the door or in any place where they could be easily gotten, and these crimes be thus committed, in these and similar cases His Holiness commanded the Archbishops, Bishops or Ordinaries and the General Superiors of Regulars to proceed according to the chapter, *De Custodia Eucharistiae* of Innocent III against such custodians of the Holy Eucharist, without delay or any other process, imposing imprisonment and any other penalties, proportioned in his judgment, to the extent of the negligence or fault, adding besides, privation of office of sacristan and, for Regulars, the privation of active or passive voice.

Moreover, if the diligence in guarding the Holy Eucharist, as outlined above, is omitted, even though no theft or sacrilege should follow, His Holiness wished that suspension from office for three months be imposed on the negligent custodian according to the cited chapter, *De Custodia Eucharistiae*. Furthermore, the parish priests and the others mentioned above were not to be excused from these penalties if the tabernacle door was left open or the keys left in an unsafe place by another priest. The custodians of the Blessed Sacrament were to be at all times alert in seeing that It was protected from all dangers of irreverence. The priests, however, who left the door of the tabernacle open or left the keys carelessly about, were also to be punished for their negligence in this matter, since they also gave occasion to the danger of irreverence by their action.

To insure the observance of all this in every case, the Bishops were given cumulative jurisdiction together with the Superiors of Regulars or exempt Religious in proceeding against the subjects of the latter guilty of this negligence.

It was made an indispensable part of the pastoral solicitude that the Ordinaries inform the Sacred Congregation of the procedure following from the above-mentioned causes.

Finally, it was ordered that the Bishops have a copy of this letter placed in all sacristies in order that parish priests and others may diligently guard the Blessed Sacrament.[44]

These decrees show with what care the Church required that the Holy Eucharist be kept from all danger of irreverence and sacrilege. The tabernacle was to be kept securely locked at all times and no one but the priest in charge of the Blessed

44. *Fontes*, n. 1868; Bizzari, *Coll. in Usum Secr. S. C. Epp. et Reg.* p 31.

Sacrament could keep the key of it. He was responsible for anything that might happen from neglect in keeping the key from others and it could not be left in a place easily accessible even though no theft or sacrilege followed.

Nevertheless, a custom continued in many places in virtue of which the key of the tabernacle was kept by others than a priest. This was especially the case in convents to which no resident chaplain was assigned. An indult, quoted by Gasparri, allowed this practice in the territory of a certain Vicar Apostolic.[45] The continuance of this custom before the Code was permitted as long as the tabernacle key was carefully guarded by the sister-sacristan and there was no official condemnation of it by the Holy See.[46]

The Code requires that the key of the tabernacle be diligently guarded but does not seem to require that it be kept personally by the priest who has charge of the church or oratory. He is responsible for its safe keeping but is not forbidden to entrust it to another for this purpose. Therefore, it may be left in the sacristy of a convent chapel if it is known that there is no danger of any irreverence following from this. It is, however, forbidden to nuns to keep the tabernacle key within the cloister.[47]

---

45. *De SS. Eucharistia*, II, p. 266.

46. Gasparri, op. cit. II, p. 267; Cappello, De Visitatione SS. Liminum, I, p. 157.

47. May 11, 1878, ad IV, Decr. Auth., n. 3448 ad IV; Vermeersch-Creusen, *Epitome*, II, p. 346; Blat. *Comm. Text. Cod. Jur. Can.* l. III, pars III, pp. 166-167; Woywod, "Law of the Code on the Divine Cult," art. *The Tabernacle*, in *The Homiletic and Pastoral Review*, vol. XXVII, p. 152.

Canon 1270. *Particulae consecratae, eo numero qui infirmorum et aliorum fidelium communioni satis esse possit, perpetuo conserventur in pyxide ex solida decentique materia, eaque munda et suo operculo bene clausa, cooperta albo vel serico et, quantum res feret, ornato.*

Canon 1272. *Hostiae consecratae, sive propter fidelium communionem, sive propter expositionem sanctissimi Sacramenti, et recentes sint et frequenter renoventur, veteribus rite consumptis, ita ut nullum sit periculum corruptionis, sedulo servatis instructionibus quas Ordinarius loci hac de re dederit.*

CHAPTER VI.

THE METHOD OF RESERVING THE BLESSED SACRAMENT.

I. THE PYX AND LUNULA

THE vessels in which the Holy Eucharist was reserved in the early centuries of the Church, were given various names by the ecclesiastical writers. St. Cyprian writes of fire coming out of an *arca* in which the Body of the Lord was contained, when touched by a woman with unclean hands.[1] St. Ambrose speaks of his brother binding the Holy Eucharist in a stole, and wearing it about his neck when threatened with ship-wreck while on a journey.[2] The *First Roman Ordo* calls the Eucharistic vessel the *capsa*.[3] The same term was used to designate these vessels in the decrees of some of the provincial councils of the Middle Ages.[4]

Another name for the vessels in which the Blessed Sacrament was reserved was that of *custodia*. This name was also applied to the tabernacle and the ostensorium.[5] Other names used were *conditorium, repositorium, sacrarium, capsula, copa, cophinus, cupa, hostiaria, loculum, suspensio, turris, and vas*.[6]

A very commonly used vessel for the reservation of the Blessed Sacrament was shaped like a dove from which it took its name of *columbarium*. Usually of gold or silver, it had an opening on the back of the figure in which the Holy Eucharist was put. It was equipped with small symetrically arranged

1. *De Lapsis*, c. XXVI, n. 4; *Corpus Scriptorum Ecclesiasticorum Latinorum*, III, p. 256; Smith-Cheetham, *Dictionary of Christian Antiquity*, II, p. 1786, art. *Reservation*.
2. *De Excessu Fratris*, 1. I; Migne, *P. L.* XVI, 1304.
3. n. 8, Muratori, *Liturgia Romana Vetus*, II, 978.
4. Conc. Oxoniense, Can. XLI, de Sacr. Altaris, Mansi, XXII, 1175; Synodal Constitutions of Odo, Bishop of Paris, cap. V, n. 8, Mansi, XXII, 678.
5. Cavalieri, *Rituale Expensum*, p. 235.
6. Corblet, *Histoire du Sacrement de L'Eucharistie*, I, p. 560, II, p. 288.

loops to which the chains, by which it was hung from the baldachin, were attached.[7]

From the very earliest days, however, mention is made of the pyx or what is quite generally called the *ciborium*. As far back as the First Council of Tours (461), there is a law requiring that priests in that province have a pyx worthy of so great a Sacrament.[8]

The word *ciborium* has had various meanings, sometimes referring to the baldachin over the altar,[9] or to the tabernacle, as it is used even today in Italy.[10] The word *pyx* has always been used to designate the vessels in which the Blessed Sacrament is kept.

In former times, various materials were used in making the pyx. Among them were alabaster, crystal, glass, tin, copper, wood, ivory, marble, silver and gold. In practically all cases, however, the interior of the pyx was plated with gold.[11]

For a while all materials were forbidden except silver or gold in the making of pyxes. Some of the other materials were forbidden to be used because of their weight, others because of the ease with which they could be broken and still others because they hastened the corruption of the Sacred Species.[12]

Silver and gold, besides being most serviceable and because of their value, are more becoming and worthy of this great Sacrament. But on August 31, 1867, the Sacred Congregation of Rites allowed the use of copper in the making of pyxes, provided the interior of the cup was gold-plated.[13]

It was forbidden to make the pyx of glass because of the ease with which it is broken and the danger of irreverence to the Blessed Sacrament.[14] The Sacred Congregation of Bishops and Regulars on July 26, 1588, forbade the use of ivory pyxes.[15]

Besides these materials, there are no others that are now

---

7. Corblet, *op. cit.* II, p. 306; Martigny, *Dictionnaire*, v. *Colombe Eucharistique*, p. 188.

8. Cap. IV, Mansi, VII 950; cf. also Council of York, (1195), can. I, Mansi, XXII, 653.

9. Martigny, *op. cit.* v. *Colombe Eucharistique*, p. 188.

10. Cavalieri, *Rituale Expensum*, p. 235; Corblet, *op. cit.* I, p. 560.

11. Can. III, Mansi, IX, 795, 806; Cap. V, n. 1, XXII, 677; Corblet, *op. cit.* II, pp. 288-292.

12. Schmalzgrueber, p. III, tit. XLIV, n. 11.

13. Decr. Auth., n. 3162 ad VI.

14. S. R. C., Jan. 30, 1880, Decr. Auth., n. 3511.

15. Martinucci, *Manuale Decretorum*, p. 76, note 1.

prohibited and all that is required is that the material be solid and becoming.[16]

In the early development of the pyx, various designs were used in fashioning them.[17] The general outlines of the designs in general use today are admirably given by St. Charles Borromeo. His description has all the features of utility as well as of beauty. He would have it be of gold or silver, and, in case it is silver, the interior of the cup should be gold-plated. The stem of the pyx should be at least six inches long so that it may be easily and firmly held. The node, becomingly ornamented, should be three inches from the base of the stem and should not be so large or so ornamented as to make the holding of the pyx inconvenient, especially when it is to be used in the giving of Holy Communion during Mass. The cup of the pyx is to be round or oval in shape and there should be due proportion between the depth of the cup and its diameter. The greater the diameter is, the deeper the cup of the pyx is to be. In the bottom of the cup there should be a semi-spherical elevation so that the last particles may be easily removed. The cover of the pyx, shaped somewhat like a cone, should correspond to the shape of the cup and should fit it snugly. It should not be so tight that it can be removed only with great difficulty and with the danger that some of the particles may be dropped. It is sufficiently well-fitted if it keeps moisture and dust out of the cup. The cover is to be surmounted by a cross or the image of our Lord.[18]

The pyx is to be covered with a white silk veil, to be ornamented becomingly. The use of these veils finds its origin in the veils that covered the vessels that were suspended over the altar when that practice was followed.[19] Suitable adornment would be painting or embroidery of figures referring to the Eucharistic Presence, as for example reproductions of the symbols found in the Catacombs.[20] The veil of the pyx, to be becoming, should be made to fit it properly.

There was in former times a dispute as to whether or not

---

16. Woywod, "Law of the Code on Divine Cult," art. *Tabernacle*, in *The Homiletic and Pastoral Review*, XXVII, p. 152.

17. Corblet, *op. cit.* II, pp. 294-313.

18. *Instr. Suppell. Eccl.*, lib. II, in Acta Eccl. Mediol., pars IV, p. 634.

19. Cap. V, Mansi, VIII, 369, Arverne, can. VII, Mansi, VIII, 861.

20. Corblet, *op. cit.* II, pp. 313-314.

the pyx should be consecrated. The chief reasons for denying the necessity of consecration were found in the fact that in the *Pontificale Romanum* and the *Rituale Romanum* the only formula for the pyx is one of blessing and not of consecration. Besides, the pyx is mentioned among the things that do not need annointing with chrism.[21]

At present, the discussion is concerned with the obligation to bless the pyx before using it. The Code says nothing on the matter and the only decree in regard to it did not give a definite answer to the question. The answer given, however, seems to add weight to the argument of those holding that it should be blessed. The question asked the Sacred Congregation of Rites was: *An et quando benedicenda sint pixis, purificatoria, ostensoria, vel saltem lunula, quae immediate inserviunt Sacramento plusquam alia: quae habent in Missali propriam formam benedictionis?* The answer was: *Servandae sunt Rubricae.*[22] This answer is considered to add force to the opinion maintaining that the pyx must be blessed, because the opinion is based on this rubric of the Missal: *Si est consecraturus plures hostias pro Communione facienda, quae ob quantitatem super patenam manere non possint, locat eas super corporale ante calicem. aut in aliquo calice consecrato, vel vase mundo benedicto.*[23]

This rubric of placing the Particles to be consecrated in a blessed vessel if the other alternatives are not used, cannot be observed as the decree requires unless the pyx is blessed. This argument, according to St. Alphonsus, makes this opinion the more probable of the two on the question.[24] The other opinion is that the pyx need not be blessed simply because there is no express obligation to do so. And in fact, there is no decree requiring it. St. Alphonsus grants to this opinion only extrinsic probability because of the authors that defend it, among whom is Suarez.[25]

With this probability in each opinion, surely no obligation can be urged to bless the pyx, but there can be no doubt that it is certainly more becoming that it should be blessed especially as the Ritual contains a formula for this. It is the same as that for

21. St. Alphonsus, *Theol. Mor.*, 1. VI, n. 384.
22. Nov. 16, 1649, ad V, Decr. Auth., n. 926.
23. *Ritus Servandae in Celebr. Missae,* tit. III, n. 3.
24. *Theol. Mor.* 1. VI, p. 385; Cappello: *De Sacramentis,* I. p. 276
25. *Opera Omnia,* XXI. disp. 81, sec. 7. n. 5.

the blessing of tabernacle.[26] The minister of this blessing are all those mentioned in Canon 1304.

The lunula in which the large Host for exposition is kept, is generally to be of gold or silver or of other suitable material as is required for the pyx. It is to be made of two circular pieces of the metal, joined at one point by a hinge, and so fitted that the Host may be firmly held in place. The lunula may be faced with glass as long as it is so arranged that the Sacred Host does not touch it. The Sacred Congregation of Rites has expressly forbidden the use of lunulae in which the Host was held in place by the glass.[27]

The use of a crescent-shaped lunula is not becoming because of the danger there is that some particles falling from the Host would be lost.[28]

What was said on the blessing of the pyx is to be applied also to the lunula.

II. THE NUMBER AND THE RENEWAL OF THE SACRED SPECIES

The number of consecrated Particles to be reserved must be sufficient for the needs of the sick and the faithful in general. The number will vary in different parishes and can only be judged from the average frequency of calls upon the priests to attend the sick and dying and to administer Holy Communion. The Blessed Sacrament is always to be kept in the pyx and under no circumstances can it be kept on the floor of the tabernacle or wrapped in the corporal.[29]

The consumption of the Sacred Species at certain intervals of time to avoid the danger of corruption and their replacement by fresh Particles has been the subject of much legislation because of the irreverence there would be if the Species were allowed to desintegrate. It is most unbecoming that the Divine Presence in the Blessed Sacrament should cease in this way. In many early provincial Councils the exact time within which the Blessed Sacrament was to be renewed was definitely deter-

26. Rit. Rom., tit. VIII, n. 23.

27. Jan. 14, 1898; Decr. Auth., n. 3974; Feb. 4, 1871, ad, IV, n. 3234

28. Van der Stappen, *Sacra Liturgia*, IV, p. 129.

29. Feb. 17, 1881, Decr. Auth., n. 3527.

mined. Not only that, but severe penalties were meted out to those who permitted the corruption of the Sacred Species. The Council of Bourges, in 1031, ordered that the Blessed Sacrament be renewed every Sunday, the older Particles to be consumed by the priest before the ablutions at Mass.[30] The same frequency was required in the renewal of the Sacred Species by so many other Councils that it may be said that the practice was almost general to renew them every week.[31]

On March 6, 1254, Innocent IV in his letter *Sub Catholicae* to the Latin and Greek bishops of the Island of Cyprus, forbade the Greeks to reserve the Blessed Sacrament consecrated on Holy Thursday, for the rest of the year and required Its renewal every fifteen days.[32]

Clement VIII, in his Instruction *Sanctissimus* of August 31, 1595, to the Italo-Greeks wrote: *Sanctissimum Eucharistiae Sacramentum, quod pro infirmis asservatur, singulis octo diebus, aut saltem quindecim removetur.*[33] He also renewed the prohibition of keeping the Blessed Sacrament for a year from one Holy Thursday to the next. These same regulations were repeated by Benedict XIV in his Constitution *Etsi Pastoralis* of May 26, 1742.[34] These declarations were, however, for the Greek Church exclusively. But similar regulations were made for the Latin Church by the Sacred Congregation of Bishops and Regulars. In a decree of August 3, 1573, it declared that the renewal of the Blessed Sacrament was to take place every Sunday and in no case was it to be extended beyond fourteen days.[35] The *Caeremoniale Episcoporum* places it among one of the chief cares of the Bishop to see that the Sacred Species are renewed at least once a week.[36]

A custom of renewing the Sacred Species every two or four weeks contrary to the prescriptions of the *Caeremoniale* was forbidden by the Sacred Congregation of Rites in the answer to this question: *In ecclesiis huius dioecesis N. servari ne potest*

30. *Item quia Corpus Domini per ecclesias paroecianas dicebatur nimia vetustate neglectum, statuerunt episcopi in eodem concilio, ut corpus Domini non plus servetur quam a Dominica in alteram,* Mansi: XIX, 503.

31. Tours, (461), cap. IV, Mansi: VII, 900; Orleans, (511), cap. IV, Mansi: VIII, 364; Godin, apud Mansi: XX, 36 & 41.

32. §3, n. 9, Fontes, n. 34.

33. §2, *Fontes,* n. 179.

34. §VI, nn. III-V, Fontes, n. 328 cf. *Allatae Sunt,* §29, Fontes, 434.

35. Fontes, n. 1308.

36. 1. I, c. VI, n. 2.

consuetudo renovandi Sanctissimam Eucharistiam semel vel bis in mense; licet qualibet hebdomada iuxta Caeremoniale Episcoporum eadem Sanctissima Eucharistia foret renovanda? The answer was: *Servetur dispositio Caeremonialis Episcoporum lib. I, c. VI, n. 2.*[37]

The Code requires nothing more than that the Sacred Species be renewed frequently. This frequency, together with other regulations on the matter, may be determined by the local Ordinary. In determining the time for the renewal of the Blessed Sacrament, the chief factors to be considered are the temperature and the climate. The Sacred Species corrupt more quickly in a climate that is damp and warm than in one that is dry and cool.[38]

The many declarations of the Holy See are to be taken into consideration also in this matter as a safe norm as to what is the outside time-limit in regard to frequency in the renewal of the Blessed Sacrament. None of them allows the renewal to be put off for more than two weeks. And not only must the time set not be such as will just barely prevent the *actual* corruption of the Hosts but must be set so as to prevent even the *danger of corruption*.[39]

For our country the Second Council of Baltimore seriously inculcated on all priests to observe faithfully the prescriptions of the *Caeremoniale Episcoporum* that the Sacred Species be renewed at least once a week.[40] It is evident that in a country as large as this the great diversity of climate will necessitate a variety of regulations on this matter. In no case however should the renewal of the Sacred Species be put off for more than two weeks.

The reason for the renewal of the Sacred Species, namely, the removal of the danger of corruption, requires that the particles with which they are replaced should be of a more recent baking. If the renewal of the Sacred Species was to be made by the consecration of Particles of the same baking as these, then there would be no need for the renewal.[41] At the same time there

---

37. Decr. Auth., n. 3621 ad II.
38. Van der Stappen, *Sacra Liturgia*, IV, p. 135.
39. Blat, *op. cit.* l. III, pars III, p. 169; Vermeersch-Creusen, *Epitome*, II, p. 347.
40. Conc. Balto., II, tit. V, cap. IV, n. 268.
41. Van der Stappen: *op. cit.* IV, pp. 136-137.

is no definite regulation in the general law of the Church stating what hosts can be called recent as the Canon requires. The Sacred Congregation of the Sacraments condemned the custom of putting in a supply of hosts to last for two or three months, and ordered the observance of the prescriptions of the Code and the Ritual.[42]

All that the Ritual says is that the Hosts or Particles to be consecrated should be fresh.[43] The Code makes the same regulation and in prescribing the use of a fresh Host for Mass it adds *ut nullum sit periculum corruptionis.*[44]

Nothing more definite than this can be found on this matter in the general law of the Church. In fact, it is next to impossible for the Church to make a definite decision. The effect that climate has on the Particles and the existence of the Church in all climates opposes any uniformity of discipline. It can only be left to the decision of each Bishop in his diocese to determine, how long the Hosts may be reasonably kept before there is danger of corruption.

The importance of care in the matter is evident from the fact that if the words of consecration are pronounced over matter that is corrupt, there is no Sacrament consecrated.[45] And if corruption has begun to set in, the celebrant is guilty of grievous sin.[46] Hence the reason that the Church requires that the Hosts to be consecrated should be fresh so as to remove even the danger of corruption.

Furthermore, as the Real Presence of Christ remains in the Holy Eucharist only so long as the Species remain incorrupt,[47] care must be taken that, if it is forseen that the consecrated Species will be kept for the whole time allowed by the regulations of the diocese, the danger of corruption within that time is removed by consecrating Particles that will remain intact during that period. The time of the renewal of the Species depends on the time the Hosts were baked, not on the time they were consecrated.[48]

In renewing the Sacred Species, the older ones are to be

---

42. Dec. 7, 1918, A. A. S. XI, p. 8.
43. Tit. IV, cap. I, *de sanctissimo Eucharistiae sacramento*, n. 7
44. Canon 815 §1
45. Missale Romanum, *De Defectibus*, III, n. 1.
46. Id., *loc. cit.* n. 3.
47. Conc. Trid., sess. XIII, *de Eucharistia*, can. 2.
48. Gasparri, *op. cit.*, II p. 276.

distributed to the faithful or consumed by the celebrant at Mass. The new hosts are not to be put in with the others unless the latter are few in number and it is certain that they will be given in Holy Communion first.[49]

This evidently applies where the Hosts are renewed only because they have been kept for the whole time that is allowed. In large parish churches, especially where those who receive Holy Communion frequently are very numerous, and the Hosts of one baking last no more than two or three weeks, it is not necessary that the Hosts consecrated first be consumed first nor that there be no mixing the hosts of one and the same baking consecrated at different times. All are of equal age and the danger of corruption is equally remote for all. When there is question of consecrating Hosts of a more recent baking than those already consecrated, the older ones should be consumed first. . Before putting newly conscerated Hosts into the pyx, the celebrant should remove all particles that may be remaining it it.

No method of purifying the ciborium is prescribed by the rubrics. Among the many ways to do this, the first of the following is the more certain and convenient in obtaining the best results.

(1). After consuming the Precious Blood, the celebrant diligently removes as many of the Particles from the pyx as he can with the forefinger ?nd thumb of his right hand. He then receives the wine of the first ablution in the pyx and slowly tilts it around the inside of cup and then pours it into the chalice from which he consumes it. He does the same with the wine and water of the second ablution and then dries the chalice and pyx with the purificator.

(2). Another method is to proceed as above with the exception that only the first ablution is received in the pyx.

(3). A third way is to remove the particles from the pyx either before or after consuming the Precious blood and receiving only the second ablutions in the pyx.

(4). A fourth method is to purify the pyx without taking any of the ablution in the pyx. This method suffices if the

---

49. Canon 1272: Gasparri, *op. cit.*, II, pp. 276-277; Cappello, *De Sacramentis*, I, p. 284.

celebrant uses all care morally possible so to collect and consume all the Particles.[50]

If for some reason it should happen that the Sacred Species do become corrupt entirely, they are to be burnt and the ashes put in the sacrarium together with the water with which the pyx is to be washed. If they are only partially corrupt and can be consumed without repugnance, they should be consumed. If they cause any repugnance, they are to be kept until they are totally corrupt and then disposed of as noted.[51]

It would be the greatest of irreverences to allow the Sacred Species to corrupt from carelessness and negligence. It is interesting and instructive to note some of the penalties that were dealt out to those who might permit this and which were established by some of the early provincial councils. The severity of these penalties will indicate the seriousness with which they regarded this crime. The Council of Orleans (511) anathematized those who kept the Sacred Species until they became mildewed and then burnt them.[52]

If the Sacrifice, i. e., the Blessed Sacrament, was so neglected that worms got into It, the one responsible for this was to do penance on bread and water for one hundred days. In such a case, the Sacrifice was to be burnt and the ashes placed under the altar, and penance was to be done for making this necessary.[53]

In the *Excerpts* taken from the Fathers and the Councils by Pope Gregory III, (731), a penance of thirty days is to be done for allowing the Sacred Species to lose their taste and color, and twenty days penance for allowing worms to get into them. In both cases, the Species are to be burned.[54]

In the *Excerpts of the Penitential* of Egbert, Archbishop of York, it is established that one neglecting the Holy Eucharist so that It becomes corrupt or losses It form, must do penance for forty days and the Hosts are to be burned.[55]

These were no light penalties and prove with what care it was always desired that the Blessed Sacrament should be guarded. The Code has not omitted to provide for the punish-

---

50. Cappello, *op. cit.*, I, p. 285.
51. Cappello, *op. cit.*, pp. 285-286.
52. Mansi, VIII, 364.
53. Ibid.
54. Can. XXVII Mansi, XII, 294; cf Arles (524), Mansi, VIII, 628.
55. Mansi, XII, 455; cf. also *Canones de Remedia Peccatorum*, can. XIII, Mansi, XII, 496.

ment for negligence in this matter as well as in all others regarding the reservation of the Blessed Sacrament as will be seen presently.

Canon 1271. *Coram tabernaculo, in quo sanctissimum Sacramentum asservatur, una saltem lampas diu noctuque continenter luceat, nutrienda oleo olivarum vel cera apum; ubi vero oleum olivarum haberi nequeat, Ordinarii loci prudentiae permittitur ut aliis oleis commutetur, quantum fieri potest, vegetabilibus.*

CHAPTER VII

THE SANCTUARY LAMP

THE final requirement for the proper reservation of the Holy Eucharist is that at least one lamp be kept burning before It continually night and day. This practice goes back as far the days of the Catacombs where there are still to be found Eucharistic towers with bronze lamps attached to them.[1] But the first legislation in regard to them is found in a decree of the Council of Verdun held in the sixth century. This decree required that a lamp be kept burning night and day before the Blessed Sacrament.[2]

In some cases candles were used instead of the lamp.[3]

A Council of Saumur (1276) required that a lamp be kept burning before the Blessed Sacrament day and night if the income of the church permitted it. In any case it was to be kept burning during the night.[4] This dependence of the obligation of keeping a light continually burning before the Blessed Sacrament on the income of the churches existed throughout the Middle Ages.[5]

However the first general law in regard to lights and the Blessed Sacrament was a decree of Pope Honorius III prescribing that when the Blessed Sacrament is taken to the sick a light is to be carried before It.[6]

The force of the general custom of keeping the lamp burning before the Blessed Sacrament reserved on the altar was given its first confirmation in a decree of the Sacred Congregation of Rites on March 23, 1593. Among the conditions set down in the indult to Rudolph, Baron of Boluailler, for the reservation of the Blessed Sacrament in a chapel he had built,

---

1. Corblet, *Histoire du Sacrement de L'Eucharistie*, II, pp. 432-433.
2. Migne, *Theologiae Cursus Completus*, XX, 310; Corblet, *loc. cit.*
3. Corblet, *loc. cit.*
4. Mansi, XXIV, 160.
5. Corblet, *op. cit.* II, 433.
6. C. 10, X, *de celebratione missarum, et sacramento Eucharistiae, et divinis officiis*, III, 41.

was that a lamp be kept burning perpetually before the tabernacle. *Dummodo ibi lampas perpetuo accensa habeatur.*[7]

In the beginning of the seventeenth century, the obligation of having a lamp burning before the Blessed Sacrament was expressly contained in the *Caeremoniale Episcoporum* and in the *Rituale Romanum*. The former had this regulation: *Lampades quoque ardentes numero impari in ecclesiis adsint, tum ad cultum et ornatum, tum ad mysticum sensum, ut et multa ex superius narratis pertinent. Hae vero in primis adhibendae sunt ante altare, vel locum ubi asservatur Sanctissimum Sacramentum, et ante altare maius, quibus in locis lampadarios pensiles esse decet, plures sustinentes lampades, ex quibus, qui ante altare maius erit, tres ad minus; qui ante Sacramentum, saltem quinque lucernas habeat.*[8] The first edition of the *Roman Ritual* says: *Lampades coram eo (tabernaculo) plures, vel saltem una, die noctuque perpetuo colluceat.*[9]

At least one lamp, therefore, must be kept burning night and day before the tabernacle of the Blessed Sacrament. In cathedrals a larger number of lamps was required for the sake of the greater splendor and veneration to be shown to the Blessed Sacrament as well as in everything else, pertaining to the worship of God. If more than one lamp is used the number had, must be an odd number. As to how great this number should be nothing more than a relative estimate may be made. If there are lamps burning elsewhere in the church before the statues or relics of the saints, the number before the Blessed Sacrament should be greater than before any other object of devotion.[10]

Since the purpose of the lamp is to call the attention of the faithful to the very center of Catholic worship, it should be prominently displayed.[11] It must be within the sanctuary and near the altar.[12]

The Sacred Congregation of Rites was asked if the lamp could be placed over the door of the chapel, opposite the altar so that the same lamp might light the corridor of an adjoining

---

7. Decr. Auth., n. 31.
8. L. I, c. XII, n. 17; cf. c. VI, n. 2.
9. Tit. IV, cap. 1, *de sanctissimo Eucharistiae sacramento*, n. 6.
10. Pignatelli, *Consultationes Canonicae*, tom. IX, cons. XC, p. 251.
11. Cavalieri, *Rituale Expensum*, pp. 231-232.
12. Van der Stappen, *Sacra Liturgia*, IV, p. 132.

monastery while little if any light penetrated the chapel, or should the lamp be placed near the altar. The Sacred Congregation replied: *Negative; et omnino lampadem esse retinendum intra et ante altare Sanctissimi Sacramenti, ut continuo ardeat. Et ita decrevit et servari mandavit.*[13]

The lamp need not be suspended from the ceiling. This was recommended as becoming by the *Caeremoniale Episcoporum* but not commanded. It is expressly allowed to use a lamp held on a bracket on the wall of the sanctuary.[14] It may not be kept on the altar nor behind the altar nor suspended directly above the table of the altar. This latter prohibition was made by the Sacred Congregation of Rites: *Permitti ne possunt in ecclesiis lumina ex oleo, quae mensae altaris imminent et ardent etiam tempore Sacrificii? Et S. R. C. respondere censuit: Negative.*[15]

Though this decree does not speak expressly of the lamp to be kept burning before the Blessed Sacrament, nevertheless, in as much as the question was asked of oil lamps in general, it includes the sanctuary lamp in which, as a rule oil is burned. Moreover, St. Charles Borromeo would not even have the lamp hang over the predella, or altar steps, in order that the priest and his server might not be disturbed by any oil that might drip from it. It should also hang not less than seven feet from the floor and more than that if the size of the church warrants it.[16]

The glass of the lamp may be any color. Thus the Holy See answered in the affirmative to the question: *Num tolerari possit usus adhibendi huiusmodi lampades ex vitro non pellucido et diaphano, sed colore aliquo tincto v. g. viridi vel rubro?*[17]

In the older editions of the Ritual nothing was said on what was to be burned in the lamp. However, the general practice was to burn olive oil though in some places candles were used. The Sacred Congregation of the Council in a decree of August 12, 1604, while making provision for the obtaining of funds necessary for the proper reservation of the Blessed

13. Aug. 22, 1699, Decr. Auth., n. 2033.

14. June 2, 1883, ad IV, Decr. Auth., n. 3576

15. June 20, 1899 ad IV, Decr. Auth., n. 4035 Cappello, *De Sacramentis*, I, p. 297; Van der Stappen, *Sacra Liturgia*, IV, p. 132-133.

16. *Instr. de Fabr. Eccl.*, 1. I, cap. XVIII, in Acta Eccl. Mediol., pars IV, p. 577.

17. June 2, 1883 ad V, Decr. Auth., n. 3576

Sacrament, mentions the lamp but does not say what is to be used in it.[18]

Several provincial councils required olive oil or candles, as was seen in the beginning of this chapter. St. Charles Borromeo ordered the same thing for his Archdiocese.[19] It was only when olive oil could not be obtained that he allowed the use of other oils.[20]

The reasons for the use of olive oil were thus put forth in the *votum consultoris* for the first decree that was given on this matter and which will be quoted presently. The constant use of olive oil in the Church can find its inspiration in the Old Testament, and notably in Exodus XXV, 6; XXVII, 20; and Leviticus XXIV, 2. There are also the mystical significations of peace and that Christ is the King of Peace. On the other hand, other oils lacked this symbolism and petroleum could not be burned because of the danger of fire or explosion. However, relying on the authority of St. Charles Borromeo in the passage quoted, he suggested that only in similar circumstances should oils other than that of olives be allowed, always giving the preference to vegetable oils.[21]

This suggestion as to the substitution of other oils for that of olives when the latter could not be obtained, was followed in the reply to the proposed doubt: *Nonnulli Reverendissimi Galliarum Antistites, serio pendentes in multis suarum dioecesium ecclesiis difficile admodum et nonnisi magnis sumptibus comparari posse oleum olivarum ad nutriendam diu noctuque saltem unam lampadem ante Sanctissimum Eucharistiae Sacramentum, ab Apostolica Sede declarari petierunt num in casu, attentis difficultatibus et ecclesiarum paupertate, oleo olivarum substitui possint alia olea, quae ex vegetabilibus habentur, ipso non excluso petroleo.*

Sacra porro Rituum Congregatio, etsi semper sollicita, ut etiam in hac parte, quod usque ab Ecclesiae primordiis circa usum olei ex olivis inductum est, ob mysticas significationes retineatur; attamen silentio praeterire minime censuit rationes ab iisdem

18. Petra. *Comm. ad Const. Apost. III*, ad Const. I Urbani IV, n. 27, Gasparri. *De SS, Eucharistia*, II. p. 273.

19. *Instr. de SS. Eucharistia*, pars *de Custodia SS. Euch.*, in Acta Eccl. Mediol., pars IV, p. 513.

20. Ibid.

21. Muhlbauer. *Decreta Authentica* S. R. C., II, pp. 432-434.

Episcopis prolatas; ac proinde, exquisito prius voto alterius ex Apostolicarum Caeremoniarum Magistris, subscriptus Cardinalis Praefectus eiusdem Sacrae Congregationis rem omnem proposuit in Ordinariis Comitiis ad Vaticanum hodierna die habitis.

Eminentissimi et Reverendissimi Patres Sacris tuendis Ritibus praepositi, omnibus accurate perpensis et diligentissime examinatis, rescribendum censuerunt: Generatim utendum esse oleo olivarum; ubi vero haberi nequeat, remittendum prudentiae Episcoporum ut lampades nutraintur ex aliis oleis, quantum fieri possit vegetabilibus.

Facta postmodum de praemissis Sanctissimo Domino nostro Pio Papae IX per infrascriptum Secretarium fideli relatione, Sanctitas Sua sententiam Sacrae Congregationis ratam habuit et confirmavit. Die 14 *Julii,* 1864.[22]

The words of the canon are taken almost verbatim from the concession in this decree. Ordinarily, therefore, today olive oil is to be burned in the sanctuary lamp. The only reasons excusing from the use of it are the difficulty in getting it or the poverty of the church that does not permit the outlay necessary to obtain it.[23]

The decision on the existence of either of these reasons, in a particular case, is left entirely to the local Ordinaries. In substituting other oils for olive oil, preference is always to be given to vegetable oils and only when even these can not be obtained petroleum can be used in the sanctuary lamp.[24]

It is also allowed to burn bees-wax candles for the sanctuary lamp. And since it is allowed to use either olive oil or candles, a composition of both is also permitted for the lamp.[25] Moreover, in the absence of olive oil, the Bishop may allow the use of candles that have a percentage of bees-wax equivalent to that required in the candles for Mass.[26]

Until 1916, the use of electricity for the illumination of the sanctuary lamp was strictly forbidden.[27] But on February 23, 1926, this decree was issued by the Sacred Congregation of Rites: *Instantibus pluribus Ordinariis locorum, in quibus ad*

---

22. Decr. Auth., n. 3121.
23. Blat, *Comm. Text. Cod. Jur Can.* 1. III, pars III, p. 168.
24. Cappello, *De Sacramentis*, I, p. 278.
25. Nov. 8, 1907, Decr. Auth., n. 4205.
26. Nov. 27, 1908, Decr. Auth., n. 4230
27. Nov. 22, 1907, Decr. Auth., n. 4206

nutriendam lampadem coram Sanctissimo Sacramento ardentem, ob peculiares circumstantias, sive ordinarias sive extraordinarias, oleum olivarum non habetur vel ob gravem penuriam aut summum pretium, non absque magna difficultate, compari potest, S. Rituum Congregatio, inhaerens decreto n. 3121, *Plurium Dioecesium, d. d.* 14 *iunii* 1864, *aliisque subsequentibus declarationibus etiam recentioribus, rescribendum censuit: 'Inspectis circumstantiis enunciatis iisque perdurantibus, remittendum prudentiae Ordinariorum, ut lampas, quae diu noctuque collucere debet coram Sanctissimo Sacramento, nutriatur, in defectu olei olivarum, aliis oleis, quantum fieri potest, vegetalibus, aut cera apum pura vel mixta, et ultimo loco etiam luce electrica adhibita; si Sanctissimo placuerit'.*

Quibus omnibus Sanctissimo Domino nostro Benedicto Papae XV per infrascriptum Cardinalem Sacrae Rituum Congregationi Pro-Praefectum relatis, Sanctitas Sua rescriptum eiusdem sacri Consilii ratum habens, quoad lampadem accensam ad Sanctissimum Sacramentum debite honorandum praescriptam, in casibus et modis superius expositis, rem omnem prudenti iudicio Ordinariorum, cum facultatibus necessariis et opportunis, benigne remisit. Contrariis non obstantibus quibuscumque.[28]

This declaration was a great concession and a wide departure from the former prohibition on the use of electric lights in the sanctuary lamp.[29] Still the Sacred Congregation was not unmindful of the earlier declarations, notably the one allowing the use of substitutes for olive oil. By this decree, electric lights could be used in case where there was great difficulty in obtaining the substitutes authorized by the former declaration.

For such a radical change from the traditional usage of the Church, there must have been some very grave reasons. An occasion of the decree may be seen in the World War which was going on when it was issued. But this condition is not expressly mentioned either as a motive for the decree or as a limitation of the time in which it could be used. The circumstances, ordinary or extraordinary, in which olive oil or the other substitutes of the earlier decree cannot be obtained because of great difficulty or the poverty of a church, may arise at any time and the electricity may be substituted. The judgment on

28. A. A. S., VIII, pp. 72-73.
29. Nov. 22, 1907, Decr. Auth., n. 4206.

whether or not the circumstances warrant this substitution is left to the Bishop.

Canon 1271 does not expressly revoke this decree and some question has arisen about the right to use it at the present time. The source of the difficulty arises from the constant practise of the Church in requiring the use of olive oil or wax candles in the sanctuary lamp, and also from the fact that this decree was issued during the War from which it is inferred that it was only a war-time measure.[30] Unless liturgicals laws are expressly changed by the Code they do not lose their force.[31] Therefore, with the decree itself containing no time limitation and with no mention of it in Canon 1271, it is possible that it may be used since there may be places where the conditions set down in it still exist.[32]

The fact that this great change in discipline happened during the war, does not by that very fact limit the time in which it could be used. Without a time limitation in the decree and with no revocation by the Code, it could be used today. Cappello unhesitatingly allows this wherever the local Ordinary may decide that the required conditions as set down in the decree, exist.[33] But Vermeersch is unwilling to make a decision and leaves the matter unsettled, pending further responses from the Sacred Congregation of Rites.[34]

The responsibility for seeing that the sanctuary lamp is kept burning day and night rests on the one who is the custodian of the Blessed Sacrament. And the lamp is to be kept clean as should everything in connection with the reservation of the Blessed Sacrament. St. Charles Borromeo would have a lamp that is used daily cleaned at least every two weeks.[35]

---

30. *Am. Eccl. Rev.* vol. LXII. pp. 457-459.
31. Canon 2.
32. Vermeersch-Creusen. Epitome, II, p. 347.
33. *De Sacramentis*, I, p. 279; cf. also Fanfani, *De Jure Religiosorum*, p. 416; Blat, *Com.* 1. III, pars III, p. 168.
34. *Epitome*, II, p. 347.
35. Conc. Prov. IV, in Acta Eccl. Mediol., pars I, p. 123.

APPENDIX I

THE RESERVATION OF THE BLESSED SACRAMENT ON HOLY THURSDAY

THE special reservation of the Blessed Sacrament on Holy Thursday for the Mass of the Pre-Sanctified on Good Friday differs in several points from the reservation of the Blessed Sacrament for the sick. To avoid the inclusion of these exceptions in the body of this work for the sake of the continuity, they have been left for an individual and brief treatment here.

After the Mass on Holy Thursday, the pyx with the Blessed Sacrament for the sick is taken from the tabernacle and placed in some more remote place in the church or preferably in the sacristy.[1]

It may not be kept in the repository with the chalice containing the large Hosts for Good Friday.[2]

Where the functions of Holy Thursday are not celebrated, the pyx with the Blessed Sacrament may be left in the tabernacle until evening for the adoration of the faithful, thus taking the place of the repository for this reason only.[3] The pyx may not be returned to the altar in the church on the evening of Good Friday.[4]

The absence of the Blessed Sacrament from the altar during these days is to be made known by leaving the door of the tabernacle open and extinguishing the sanctuary lights.[5]

In order that the Blessed Sacrament may be reserved in the repository on Holy Thursday, the following conditions are required. First, it may only be done where there is habitual

---

1. Pignatelli, *Consultationes Canonicae*, tom. IX, cons. XC, Gasparri, *De SS. Eucharistia*, II, p. 259.
2. S. R. C., Dec. 9, 1899 ad IV, Decr. Auth., n. 4049; Van der Stappen, *Sacra Liturgia*, V, quaest. 124, n. 14; Wuest, *Collectio Rerum Liturgicarum*, p. 230.
3. S. R. C., Feb. 1, 1895 ad III, Decr. Auth., n. 3842
4. S. R. C., Mar. 12, 1836 ad IV Decr. Auth., n. 2740
5. Cavalieri, *Rituale Expensum*, p. 30; Pignatelli, *loc. cit.*

reservation of the Blessed Sacrament.[6] Another condition is that the Host reserved must be consecrated at the Mass on Holy Thursday for the priest is forbidden to use a Host on Good Friday that is consecrated on any other day.[7] And if the Mass is said on Holy Thursday, the consecration of a Host for the Mass of the Pre-Sanctified is obligatory unless there is given to some one a special faculty to say Mass on Holy Thursday alone. Cardinals have the privilege of saying Mass on Holy Thursday or of having another say Mass before them.[8] Bishops can do the same if they are not bound to celebrate Mass on Holy Thursday in their Cathedral.[9]

Besides these and any others that may have this privilege in virtue of a particular indult, Mass cannot be said unless this reservation of the consecrated Hosts for Good Friday is to follow.[10]

The permission to say a low Mass can be granted by the Bishop to those pastors who can not carry out the full prescriptions of the ceremonies because of the lack of clerics. If there are three or four in a place, they are to follow the small Ritual of Benedict XIII. And if this small number cannot be had, the Bishop can allow the saying of one low Mass for the convenience of the people, though the functions of the following day are omitted.[11]

The permission according to the decrees quoted must be asked for and renewed each year. The Superior of Regulars may grant the same permission for a low Mass in their domestic oratory or in the church with the doors closed, if the full ceremonies of Holy Week cannot be carried out.[12]

For a low Mass in other churches and oratories, whether those of hospitals, seminaries, convents, etc., without the sub-

---

6. S. R. C., June 14, 1659, Decr. Auth., n. 1120.

7. S. R. C., Aug. 20, 1870, Decr. Auth., n. 3219.

8. Canon 239, §1, n. 4

9. Canon 349, §1, n. 1.

10. S. R. C. Mar. 28, 1775 ad V, Decr. Auth., n. 2503, Aug. 31, 1839 ad I, n. 2799, Dec. 9, 1899 ad I, n. 4049.

11. S. R. C. July 2, 1821 ad I, Decr. Auth., n. 2616, Feb. 1, 1895, ad II, n. 3842.

12. S. R. C., Aug. 31, 1839, Decr. Auth., n. 2799, Dec. 9, 1899 ad II, n. 4049.

sequent reservation of the Blessed Sacrament for the Mass of Good Friday, an Apostolic indult is necessary.[13]

Where there is a custom of allowing Mass in these oratories on Holy Thursday, most of the authors quoted agree that it can be continued.

The general rule, then is that the Blessed Sacrament must be consecrated at the Mass on Holy Thursday for the Mass of the Pre-Sanctified on Good Friday.

The repository where the large Host is to be kept is to be in a chapel of the church or on an altar of the church other than the main altar.[14]

The altar is to be becomingly adorned with veils, lights and flowers. But at the same time all theatrical effects are to be rigorously excluded on Holy Thursday as well as at other times in connection with the reservation of the Blessed Sacrament. Neither is it allowed to have on the altar or in the chapel of the Repository any penitential or sorrowful colors in the decorations.[15]

For, though the reservation of the Blessed Sacrament in the repository represents the burial of our Lord, it also commemorates the institution of the Blessed Sacrament and, therefore, everything must be in accordance with this happy event.[16]

In the adornment of the altar it is not allowed to use chalices, pyxes or ostensoria.[17]

Statues may not be used in the adornment of the altar of Reposition and the Bishop may enforce this decree even in the churches belonging to Regulars.[18]

Where, however, there is an ancient custom of using the statues of our Lord, the Blessed Virgin and the other saints connected with the Passion, its continuance may be tolerated

---

13. Decr. Auth., n. 4049 ad II; Wuest, *op. cit.*, p. 228; Genicot, *Theologia Moralis*, II, p. 208; Cappello; *De Sacramentis*, I, p. 643; Many, *Prael. de Missa*, p. 30; Gasparri, *op. cit.*, I, p. 48.

14. Missale Romanum, *Feria V in Coena Domini;* Decr. Auth., n. 4077 ad X.

15. S. R. C., Jan. 21, 1662, Decr. Auth., n. 1223.

16. S. R. C., Dec. 7, 1844, ad I, Decr. Auth., n. 2873, Dec. 15, 1896 ad I, n. 3939.

17. Decr. Auth., n. 4077 ad X.

18. S. R. C., Sept. 26, 1868, Decr. Auth., n. 3178, May 27, 1903, n. 4112.

by the Bishop, but it is strictly forbidden to introduce this custom in churches where it does not already exist.[19]

Where this custom is observed, the statues must conform to the facts and scenes as related in the Gospels.[20]

Veils that are used in the decoration of the altar may not be hung from the cross on the altar or over the altar and must not cover the Holy Eucharist.[21]

The *capsa* or tabernacle in which the Blessed Sacrament is to be kept is to be placed on the altar as the rubrics in the Missal for Holy Thursday prescribe. It is not to be placed on the floor in a cave-like representation of the Garden of Olives.[22]

It is also to be so constructed that the chalice cannot be seen by the people.[23]

It is not allowed to keep the pyx with the Blessed Sacrament for the sick in this tabernacle on these days.[24]

The tabernacle of the repository is to be securely locked and the key is to be kept by the priest who is to be celebrant of the functions on Good Friday.[25]

It is forbidden to give this key to any layman, whatever may be his rank or position, and any custom of doing so is an abuse to be abolished. This prohibition affects all churches, secular as well as those of regulars.[26]

Furthermore, even though the custom of giving the key of this tabernacle to the governor or prefect of the civil government was very ancient, and its abolition might cause difficulties, the most that the Sacred Congregation of Rites would allow was the giving of a symbolic key which was not to be a real key to the tabernacle.[27]

It is also forbidden to affix a seal to the door of this tabernacle to be publicly removed on Good Friday.[28]

The consecrated Host to be reserved for Good Friday is

---

19. S. R. C., Dec. 15, 1896, ad II, Decr. Auth., n. 3939.
20. S. R. C., Sept. 26, 1868, Decr. Auth., n. 3178.
21. S. R. C., Aug. 8, 1835, ad I, Decr. Auth., n. 2734.
22. S. R. C., Sept. 26, 1868 ad I, Decr. Auth., n. 3178.
23. S. R. C., Mar. 30, 1886, ad I, Decr. Auth., n. 3660.
24. S. R. C., Dec. 9, 1899 ad IV, Decr. Auth., n. 4049.
25. S. R. C., Dec. 6, 1631, Decr. Auth., n. 579; cf also nn. 635, 2335, 2830, ad I, 2833.
26. Decr. Auth., ibid.
27. S. R. C., Aug. 7, 1880, Decr. Auth., 3518.
28. S. R. C., Sept. 18, 1872, Decr. Auth., n. 2172; Dec. 7, 1844, ad I, n. 2873.

placed in the chalice by the celebrant before the ablutions of the Mass on Holy Thursday. The Deacon then covers the chalice with a pall on top of which he places an inverted paten. He then covers all with a white silk veil. After the procession arrives at the altar of Reposition the chalice with the Host is placed in the tabernacle by the Deacon and the door is locked.[29]

It is not allowed to expose the Host on the altar for the adoration of the faithful. It is to be left in the chalice in the tabernacle until the ceremonies call for its removal on Good Friday.[30]

---

29. Missale Romanum. *Feria V in Coena Domini.*
30. S. R. C., Feb. 14, 1705 ad VI, Decr. Auth., n. 2148.

APPENDIX II

PENALTIES FOR NEGLIGENCE IN THE CUSTODY OF THE BLESSED SACRAMENT

IT will be recalled that in mentioning the strict regulaions for the proper custody of the Holy Eucharist at different periods of the Church's history, the penalties set down for the punishment of offenses against different regulations were also referred to. All the procedure and the penalties for the violation of the specific laws have now been united in the punishment of any grave negligence in the custody of the Blessed Sacrament.

A pastor who is gravely negligent in the proper custody of the Holy Eucharist is to be punished according to the norms of Canons 2182-2185.[1]

The Bishop must decide that there is this grave negligence. There is no formal process to be gone through in a judicial way to prove this. The Bishop acts in these cases in his administrative capacity. When the Bishop is certain of grave negligence in the custody of the Blessed Sacrament on the part of the pastor, he is to give him a canonical warning that recalls to mind the obligations of the pastor in this matter and the penalties established by law for this crime. This warning is in itself penal, being a remedy for the prevention of the crime. It is not directly a correction.[2]

If the pastor does not correct the negligence, the Bishop is to give him a reprimand and inflict a penalty proportioned to the gravity of the negligence. Before doing this, however, he is to decide that it is certain that the negligence in a matter of grave moment in the custody of the Holy Eucharist has continued or been repeated again and again for a notable time, and without an excusing cause. To aid him in making this decision, he is to

---

1. Canon 2382.
2. Canon 2182.

consult two examiners and give the pastor an opportunity to derend himself.[3]

This correction or reprimand is to be given publicly, i. e., before a notary or two witnesses, or by letter, the contents and reception of which are to be certified by some document. This correction may be repeated by the Bishop if he sees fit.[4]

If the reprimand and the penalty inflicted with it do not bring about a correction of the negligence, after the Bishop is certain that it is still perserved in, he may proceed to the infliction of further penalties. In arriving at the proof of the continuance of the absence of correction and the lack of excuse, he is to proceed as in the former canon. The penalty of depriving a removable pastor of his parish for not correcting the negligence is not necessarily to be imposed. The Code says that he may do this. The penalty to be inflicted on an irremovable pastor is the partial or total privation of the fruits of the parish according to the nature and gravity of the negligence.[5]

If the irremovable pastor does not then correct the negligence then he is to be deprived of his parish. The same process in arriving at certainty on the perseverance in the crime is to be followed here as in the two preceding canons.[6]

These penalties are determined only for pastors negligent in the custody of the Holy Eucharist. Nothing is said in the Code expressly on the penalties to be imposed on others for negligence in this matter. They cannot be included in this term *parochus* for not only is this a penal matter and, therefore, to be restricted but it is also forbidden to extend it.[7]

It is not fitting, however, that other custodians of the Blessed Sacrament, besides the pastors, should not be punished if they should be gravely negligent in their duties in this regard. Provision is made in the Code, in virtue of which the Bishop in this case can inflict any penalties he thinks any negligence merits. Canon 2221 gives him the power to attach a penalty to any law of the Church that has none attached to it by the Holy See and

3. Canon 2183.
4. Canon 2309, §§2 & 6.
5. Canon 2184.
6. Canon 2185.
7. Canon 20.

to increase the penalties established by law. In this way the Church has provided for the proper observance of all its laws.

In closing this dissertation, no better conclusion can be found than the following words of the Ritual: *Parochus summum studium in eo ponat, ut cum ipse venerabile hoc Sacramentum qua decet reverentia, debitoque cultu tractet, custodiat et administret. . . .Curabit parochus, ut omnia ad ipsius Sacramenti cultum ordinata, integra, mundaque sint, et conserventur.*[8]

8. Tit. IV. cap. 1. *de sanctissimo Eucharistiae sacramento*, nn. 2 & 6.

SOURCES

Acta Apostolicae Sedis, vols. I—Rome, 1909.—
Acta Ecclesiae Mediolanensis, Milan, 1599.
Acta Gregorii Papae XVI, Vannutelli-Bernasconi, 4 vols., Rome, 1901.
Acta Sanctae Sedis. 41 vols., Rome, 1865- 1908.
Caeremoniale Episcoporum, Mechlin. 1867.
Codex Juris Canonici, Rome.
Codicis Juris Canonici Fontes, 4 vols., Rome, 1924-1926.
Collectanea Sacrae Congregationis de Propaganda. Fide, 2 vols., Rome, 1907.
Councilii Plenarii Baltimorensis II Acta et Decreta, Baltimore, 1868.
Corpus Juris Canonici, Editio Richter-Freidberg, Leipsic, 1922.
Dcreta Authentica Sacrae Rituum Congregationis, 6 vols., Rome, 1898-1912.
Missale Romanum, *Ratisbon*, 1921.
Rituale Romanum, Rome, 1925.
Pontificale Romanum, Rome, 1890.
Sacrosancti et Oecumenici Concilii Tridentini Canones et Decreta, Editio III, Chiffletius, Paris, 1910.

BIBLIOGRAPHY

Augustine, Charles, O. S. B., *A Commentary on the New Code of Canon Law*, 2 Ed. 8 vols., St. Louis, 1921.

Barbosa, Augustinus, *Collectanea Doctorum in Councilium Tridentum*, Lyons, 1657.

———. *Summa Apostolicarum Decisionum*, Lyons, 1658.

———. *Tractatus Varii*, Lyons, 1659.

Bargilliat, M., *Praelectiones Juris Canonici*, 31 Ed. 2 vols., Paris, 1918

Batiffol, *Etudes de Theologie Positive*, 3 Ed., Paris, 1920.

Beyerlinck, Laurentius, *Magnum Theatrum Vitae Humanum*, 7 vols., Lyons, 1665.

Bizzari, Card., *Collectanea in Usum Secretariae S. Congr. Epp. et Reg.*, 2 ed. Rome, 1885.

Blat, Albertus, O. P., *Commentarium Textus Codicis Juris Canonici*, 5 vols., Rome, 1924.

Bona, Card., *Rerum Liturgicarum*, Rome, 1671.

Bouvry, G. F. J., *Expositio Rubricarum*, 2 vols. Paris, 1864.

Braun, Joseph, S. J., *Der Christliche Altar*, Munchen, 1924.

———. *Die Liturgischen Paramente*, Freiburg, 1924.

———. *Praktische Paramentekunde*, Freiburg, 1924.

———. *Liturgisches Hanlexikon*, Regensburg.

Bridgett, *The Holy Eucharist in Great Britain*, London, 1881.

Cappello, Felix, S. J., *De Sacramentis*, 3 vols., Rome, 1921-1926.

———. *De Visitatione SS. Liminum et Dioeceseon*, 2 vols., Rome, 1912.

Catalanus, Joseph, *Caeremoniale Episcoporum Commentariis Illustratum*, 2 ed., 2 vols., Paris, 1860.

Cavalieri, John Michael *Rituale Expensum*, Bergamo, 1758.

Cienfuegos, Albaro Card., *Bibliotheca Selecta de Ritu Azymo et Fermentato*, Venice, 1729.

Corblet, Jules, *Histoire du Sacrement de L'Eucharistie*, 2 vols., Paris, 1885.

De Herdt, P. J. B., *Sacrae Liturgiae Praxis*, 5 ed. 3 vols., Louvain, 1870.

Duchesne, L. *Liber Pontificalis*, 2 vols., Paris, 1868.

Duschesne, Msgr. L., *Christian Worship: Its Origin and Evolution*. Translated from the Third French Edition by M. McLure, New York, 1903.

Eisenhofer, Ludwig, *Katolische Liturgik*, Wein.

Fanfani, Ludovicus, O. P., *De Jure Parochorum*, Rome, 1924.

Fanfani, Ludovicus, O. P., *De Jure Religiosorum*, 2 ed., Rome, 1925.

Ferraris, F. Lucius, *Prompta Bibliotheca*, 8 vols., Paris, 1885.

Freeland, Msgr. Canon. Reservation of the Blessed Sacrament, in, *Catholic Faith in the Holy Eucharist*, 2 ed., St. Louis, 1923.

Gasparri, Peter Card., *Tractatus Canonicus de SS. Eucharistia*, 2 vols., Paris, 1897.

Gatticus, John Baptist, *De Oratoriis Domesticis*, Rome, 1746.

Genicot, Eduardus, S. J., *Institutiones Theologiae Moralis*, 2 vols., 3 ed. after the Code, Brussels, 1922.

Giraldus, Ubaldus, *Expositio Juris Pontificii*, 3 vols. in 2, Rome, 1829.

Hartel, Gulielmus, *Corpus Scriptorum Ecclesiasticorum Latinorum*, *Vindobonae*, 1868.

Hedley, *The Holy Eucharist*, London, 1910.

Leech, George L. *A Comparative Study of the Constitution "Apostolicae Sedis" and the "Codex Juris Canonici."* Washington, 1922.

Liguori, St. Alphonsus Maria de. *Theologia Moralis*, 2 ed. 8 vols., Ratisbon, 1880.

Lucidi, Angelo, *De Visitatione Sacrorum Liminum*, 3 ed. 3 vols., Rome, 1883.

Mabillon, Johannis, O. S. B., *De Azymo et Fermentato*, Edition of Cienfuegos, Venice, 1729.

———. *Museum Italicum*, 2 vols., Paris, 1724.

Mansi, Johannis, *Sacrorum Counciliorum Nova et Amplissima Collectio*, 50 vols., Paris, 1902.
Many, S., SS., *Praelectiones de Missa*, Paris, 1903.
Martene, Edmund, *De Antiquis Ecclesiastiticis Ritibus*, 4 vols. Rouen. 1700-1706.
Martigny, M. L'Abbe, *Dictionnaire des Antiquites Chretiennes*, 2 ed., Paris, 1887.
Martinucci, Pius, *Manuale Decretorum*, Ratisbon, 1873.
Migne, J. P., *Patrologia Graeca*, 161 vols., Paris, 1858-1864.
——————. *Patrologia Latina*, 221 vols., Paris, 1847-1870.
——————. *Theologiae Cursus Completus*, 28 vols., Paris, 1845-1860.
Muhlbauer, Wolfgang, *Decreta Authentica S. R. C. Supplementum*, 3 vols., Munich, 1879.
Muratori, Ludovico, *Liturgia Romana Vetus*, 2 vols., Venice, 1748.
Noldin, H., S. J., *Summa Theologiae Moralis*, 16 ed., 3 vols., Innsbruck, 1923.
Pasqualigus, Zacharia, *De Sacrificio Novae Legis Quaestiones Theologicae, Morales, Juridicae*. 2 vols., Venice, 1707.
Pelella, Joseph, *Canones et Decreta Concilii Tridentini. accedunt S. Congr. Card. Conc. Trid. Interpretum Declarationes ac Resolutiones, etc.*, Naples, 1859.
Petra, Vincent Card., *Commentaria ad Constitutiones Apostolicas*, 4 vols. in 3, Venice, 1729.
Pignatelli, James, *Consultationes Canonicae*, 11 vols. in 5, Colonia Allobrogum 1700.
Probst, Ferdinand, *Sakramente und Sakramentalien in den Drei Ersten Jahrhunderten*, Tubingen, 1872.
Raible, *Der Tabernakel Einst und Jetst*, Freiburg, 1908.
Rock, Daniel, *The Church of Our Fathers*, 4 vols., London, 1903.
——————. *Hierurgia*, 2 vols., 3 ed., Revised by W. H. J. Weale, London, 1892.
Roelker, Edw. J., *Principles of Privilege*, Washington, 1926.
Rohault de Fleury, Charles, *La Messe*, 8 vols., Paris, 1883-1889.
Schmalzgrueber, Francis, S. J., *Jus Ecclesiasticum*, 12 vols., Rome, 1844.
Schulze, Frederick, *A Manual of Pastoral Theology*, 3 ed. St. Louis, 1923.
Smith-Cheetham, *A Dictionary of Christian Antiquities*, 2 vols., Hartford, 1880.
Suarez, Francis, S. J., *Opera Omnia*, 26 vols., Paris, 1866.
Van der Stappen, J. F., *Sacra Liturgia*, 2 ed., 5 vols., Mechlin, 1905.
Vermeersch, Arthur, S. J., *De Religiosis et Missionariis Supplementa et Monumenta Periodica*, 9 vols., Bruges, 1909-1919.
Vermeersch-Creusen, *Epitome Juris Canonici*, 2 ed., 3 vols., Mechlin, 1924.
Wernz, F. X., S. J., *Jus Decretalium*, 6 vols., Rome, 1901.
Wilpert, *Fractio Panis*, Freiburg, 1895.
Wuest, Joseph, C. SS. R., *Collectio Rerum Liturgicarum*, 4 ed., Boston, 1921

PERIODICALS

American Ecclesiastical Review, Vols. 1—, Philadelphia, 1889—.
Ephemerides Liturgicae, Vols. I—, Rome, 1887—.
Homiletic and Pastoral Review, The Vols. 1—, New York, 1904—.
Irish Ecclesiastical Record, The, Vols. I—, Dublin, 1865—.
Monitore Ecclesiastico, Il, Series III. Vols. 1—. Rome, 1909.

UNIVERSITAS CATHOLICA AMERICAE

WASHINGTONII, D. C.

FACULTAS JURIS CANONICI

1927

No. 40

DEUS LUX MEA

THESES

QUAS

AD DOCTORATUS GRADUM

IN

UTROQUE IURE

APUD UNIVERSITATEM CATHOLICAM AMERICAE

CONSEQUENDUM
PUBLICE PROPUGNABIT

GULIELMUS THOMAS CAVANAUGH

SACERDOS
CONGREGATIONIS PASSIONIS

IURIS UTRIUSQUE LICENTIATUS

HORA IX A.M. DIE XXV MAII A. D. MCMXXVII

EX IURE PUBLICO

I.	De Ecclesia, qua Societate Perfecta	
II.	De Forma Regiminis in Ecclesia	
III.	De Suprema Potestate in Ecclesia	
IV.	De Episcopatu	
V.	De Relatione inter Ecclesiam et Statum	
VI.	De Concordatis	

EX IURE CANONICO

VII.	De Historia Iuris Canonici ante Gratianum	
VIII.	De Corpore Iuris Canonici	
IX.	De Historia Iuris Canonici inde a Corpore Iuris Canonici usque ad Codicem Iuris Canonici	
X.	De Ipso Codice Iuris Canonici	
XI.	Normae Introductoriae.	1-6
XII.	De Legibus Ecclesiasticis	8-24
XIII.	De Consuetudine	25-30
XIV.	De Temporis Supputatione	31-35
XV.	De Rescriptis	36-62
XVI.	De Privilegiis	63-79
XVII.	De Dispensationibus	80-86
XVIII.	De Persona Physica et Morali in Ecclesia	87-91, 99-102
XIX.	De Domicilio et Quasi-domicilio	92-95
XX.	De Potestate Ordinaria et Delegata	196-210
XXI.	De Nominatione et Institutione Episcoporum	329-333
XXII.	De Iuribus et Obligationibus Episcoporum	334-349
XXIII.	De Officio Parochorum	451-454
XXIV.	De Erectione et Suppressione Religionis, Provinciae, Domus	492-498
XXV.	De Superioribus et Capitulis	499-517
XXVI.	De Confessariis et Cappellanis	518-530
XXVII.	De Bonis Temporalibus eorumque Administratione	531-537
XXVIII.	De Novitiatu	542-571
XXIX.	De Professione Religiosa	572-586
XXX.	De Obligationibus Religiosorum	592-612
XXXI.	De Privilegiis Religiosorum	613-625
XXXII.	De Subiecto Sacrae Communionis	853-866
XXXIII.	De Ministro Sacramenti Paenitentiae	871-892
XXXIV.	De Reservatione Peccatorum	893-900
XXXV.	De Natura Matrimonii	1012-1016
XXXVI.	De Impedimentis Matrimonialibus in Genere	1035-1042
XXXVII.	De Dispensatione Impedimentorum Matrimonialium	1043-1057
XXXVIII.	De Impedimentis Dirimentibus	1067-1080
XXXIX.	De Forma Celebrationis Matrimonii	1094-1103
XL.	De Matrimonii Convalidatione	1133-1141
XLI.	De Custodia Sanctissimae Eucharistiae	1265-1272
XLII.	De Voto	1307-1315
XLIII.	De Sacris Concionibus	1337-1348
XLIV.	De Foro Competenti	1556-1568
XLV.	De Officio Iudicum et Tribunalis Ministrorum	1608-1626
XLVI.	De Actore et Reo Convento	1646-1654
XLVII.	De Testibus et Attestationibus	1754-1791
XLVIII.	De Querela Nullitatis	1892-1897

ROMAN LAW

INTERNATIONAL LAW

Vidit Facultas Iuris Canonici:

PHILIPPUS BERNARDINI, S.T.D., J.U.D., Decanus.
LUDOVICUS H. MOTRY, S.T.D., J.C.D., a Secretis.
VALENTINUS T. SCHAAF, O.F.M., J.C.D.
FRANCISCUS LARDONE, S.T.D., J.U.D.
MANUEL DE OLIVIERA LIMA, L.H.B.

Vidit Rector Universitatis:

✠ THOMAS J. SHAHAN, S.T.D.

BIOGRAPHY

William Thomas Cavanaugh was born on April 22, 1899, in Dunkirk, N. Y. At the completion of his second year in High School in his native city, he entered the Passionists' Preparatory School, then located at Baltimore. In 1916, he entered the novitiate of the same Congregation and was professed the following year. After finishing his seminary course, he was ordained to the Holy Priesthood on June 14, 1924. The following January, he entered the Catholic University of America for graduate work in Canon Law.

www.ingramcontent.com/pod-product-compliance
Lightning Source LLC
LaVergne TN
LVHW050159080826
844660LV00012B/317

* 9 7 8 0 8 1 3 2 2 2 2 9 5 *